ROUTLEDGE LIBRARY EDITIONS:
ECONOMICS AND SOCIETY

Volume 29

SOCIAL CLAUSES AND INTERNATIONAL TRADE

SOCIAL CLAUSES AND INTERNATIONAL TRADE

An Economic Analysis of Labour Standards in Trade Policy

GÖTE HANSSON

Routledge
Taylor & Francis Group
LONDON AND NEW YORK

First published in 1983 by Croom Helm Ltd.

This edition first published in 2026
by Routledge
4 Park Square, Milton Park, Abingdon, Oxon OX14 4RN

and by Routledge
605 Third Avenue, New York, NY 10158

Routledge is an imprint of the Taylor & Francis Group, an informa business

British Library Cataloguing in Publication Data
A catalogue record for this book is available from the British Library

ISBN: 978-1-032-97576-4 (Set)
ISBN: 978-1-041-15621-5 (Volume 29) (hbk)
ISBN: 978-1-041-15625-3 (Volume 29) (pbk)
ISBN: 978-1-003-68040-6 (Volume 29) (ebk)

DOI: 10.4324/9781003680406

Publisher's Note
The publisher has gone to great lengths to ensure the quality of this reprint but points out that some imperfections in the original copies may be apparent.

Social Clauses and International Trade

AN ECONOMIC ANALYSIS OF LABOUR STANDARDS IN TRADE POLICY

GÖTE HANSSON

CROOM HELM
London & Canberra

ST. MARTIN'S PRESS
NEW YORK

Croom Helm Ltd, Provident House, Burrell Row,
Beckenham, Kent BR3 1AT

British Library Cataloguing in Publication Data

Hansson, Göte
Social clauses and international trade.
1. Commerce
I. Title
382 HF1007

ISBN 0-7099-1235-8

St. Martin's Press, Inc., 175 Fifth Avenue, New York, N.Y. 10010
Printed in Great Britain
First published in the United States of America in 1983

Library of Congress Cataloging in Publication Data

Hansson, Göte, 1950–
Social clauses and international trade.

Revision of the author's thesis (Ph.D) – University of Lund
Bibliography: p.
Includes index.
1. Foreign trade regulation. 2. Labor laws and legislation, International. I. Title.
K3943.H36 1982 343'.087 82-42563
ISBN 0-312-73162-0 342.387

Typeset by Leaper & Gard Ltd, Bristol
Printed and bound in Great Britain

CONTENTS

To my mother and to the memory of my father

PREFACE

The present book is a slightly revised version of my doctoral thesis presented at the University of Lund: *Lund Economic Studies*, no. 25.

The study is one of the results of the project *International Trade, Protectionism, and Social Clauses*, that was initiated in 1978 by Bengt Säve-Söderbergh at the International Centre of the Swedish Labour Movement (AIC), and Roland Svensson who at that time was the Director of the Swedish Work Life Research Centre (Arbetslivscentrum). Roland Svensson's contact with Professor Bo Södersten at the Department of Economics at the University of Lund was the starting point for my work on the project. To the initiators and other participants at the introductory seminars at the Swedish Work Life Research Centre, especially Professors Villy Bergström and Carl Hamilton, I am indeed most grateful.

The financial support received from the Swedish Work Life Research Centre has been of decisive importance for the realisation of the project and is gratefully acknowledged.

During my work on the thesis, which began in the autumn term of 1979, I have received regular support, encouragement and supervision from my supervisors, Professors Bo Södersten and Mats Lundahl, to whom I owe the greatest gratitude. I also owe many thanks to my colleague Bo Larsson who has shown enormous patience in always being available for constructive discussions when problems have arisen. The regular seminar in international economics at the Department of Economics in Lund has provided valuable help during the work on the study. Among the numerous participants in these seminars I would wish to particularly mention Lennart Petersson and Claudio Vedovato who have read and made valuable comments and suggestions on early drafts of the study. I also owe many thanks to Professor Björn Thalberg, Krister Hjalte and Maria Lagerstedt who acted as opponents at the final seminars and to Professors Ingemar Ståhl and Lars Söderström for their valuable comments in conjunction with these seminars.

Many thanks are also directed to the organisers of and the

participants in the Symposium on South-east Asia at Hasseludden, Stockholm, in 1979, that was arranged by the International Centre of the Swedish Labour Movement, and the Workshop on Production and Trade in a World of Internationally Mobile Factors of Production, financed by the Bank of Sweden Tercentenary Foundation, and held at the Institute for International Economic Studies, University of Stockholm, in 1980.

In preparing the final manuscript of this book, the comments made by Professor Lennart Jörberg and the faculty opponent Professor Victor Norman have been of great value and I am most grateful for the careful notations that Professor Norman made in conjunction with the public discussion of my doctoral thesis.

I have also received great help from Alan Harkess who has tried to turn my Swenglish into a more readable English, and from Eva Björkbom and Agnetta Kretz who have efficiently typed the manuscript and drawn the figures. For this help I am most grateful.

Many thanks are also directed to Peter Stenkula, the Head of the Department of Economics in Lund who has provided office space and an economic basis during my postgraduate studies, to Hedvig Ahlbom who has always been at hand solving practical and administrative problems and to Keith Persson who without delay has duplicated the various drafts of my work with great care.

Finally, any mistakes that remain are of course my sole responsibility.

Lund
Göte Hansson

1 INTRODUCTION

The present study deals with the question of rules of conduct in international competition and trade. Such rules may cover various fields of economic policy, such as fiscal policy, environmental policy and social policy.[1] In this study, we will concentrate on one specific area of social policy, namely labour market policy. During the 1970s, frequent demands have been made for the incorporation of labour standards, or social clauses, into the rules that govern international trade. A measure of this kind would make it possible to restrict imports of commodities that have been produced by means of working conditions that are inferior to the minimum requirements stated in the incorporated standards or clauses. Countries that do not comply with the minimum requirements must choose between a change in working conditions or run the risk of being confronted with increased trade barriers in their export markets. The economic effects of the two alternatives are assumed to have a decisive bearing on this choice. In short, the overall aim of this study is to analyse the economic effects of an incorporation of labour standards into the rules that govern international trade.

The question of labour standards and international trade is of longstanding importance and it is essential first to carry out a historical review of the demands for international labour standards, in order to give a historical perspective of the problem at hand. Section 1.2 will examine recent trade policy development, in order to give a trade policy perspective to the study and finally, a more detailed description of the aim and plan of the present study will be presented.

1.1 Labour Standards and International Trade – A Historical Review[2]

The Pioneers

The question of international labour standards and international trade has a long history. As early as the first half of the nineteenth century, international labour standards were emphasised as a means of making national labour legislation possible notwithstanding the existence of international competition.

Robert Owen, the English manufacturer and philanthropist, is often mentioned as a pioneer in international labour legislation. In 1818, Owen wrote two Memorials that were closely related to the subject, and they were presented to the Congress of the Concert of Europe at Aix-la-Chapelle in the same year.[3] However, since these Memorials are very general in their wording and do not explicitly mention international labour legislation, it is doubtful that they provide sufficient justification to allow us to consider Owen as the founder of the idea of international labour legislation.[4] According to Follows, the person who should be given this honour is Charles Frederick Hindley, who was a Member of Parliament for Ashton-under-Lyne between 1835 and 1857.[5]

In 1833, Hindley suggested a foreign treaty on labour legislation. His suggestion was based upon a clear insight into the interdependence between nations that was created by foreign trade and international competition. The working condition explicitly dealt with in Hindley's suggestion was hours of work.[6]

The trade argument for international labour legislation was also advanced by the French liberal economist Jérome Blanqui. In 1838–9, he wrote on the possibilities of avoiding the abuses of manufacturing workers by means of labour legislation:

> There is only one way of accomplishing it [the reform] while avoiding its disastrous consequences: this would be to get it adopted simultaneously by all industrial nations which compete in the foreign market. Will people be willing to do this? Can it be done? Why not? Treaties have been concluded between one country and another by which they have bound themselves to kill men; why should they not be concluded today for the purpose of preserving men's lives and making them happier?[7]

The same line of argument can be found in a lecture on child labour legislation given in France in 1868 by another liberal economist, Louis Wolowski.[8] Wolowski's lecture rests on the observed opposition to national labour legislation, an opposition that was based on the fear of losing international competitiveness.

One of the pioneers of international labour legislation, who should be given a central place, is the Alsatian manufacturer Daniel Legrand. According to Mahaim, Legrand is considered historically to be the first person who actively attempted to obtain international labour legislation.[9] Furthermore, in a recent publication from the ILO, Legrand is said to be 'the principle originator of the idea of international labour legislation, and precursor of the work of the International Labour Organisation'.[10]

Between 1838 and 1855 Legrand bombarded European governments with various memoranda on the need for international labour legislation. In the final one, which was addressed to the governments of all industrial countries, Legrand wrote:

> An international factory law has an immense advantage over national laws. It can afford moral and material benefits to the working class without prejudice to the manufacturers and without the least shock to international competition.[11]

The first person who suggested the establishment of an international labour organisation was, according to Follows, Edouard Ducpétiaux from Belgium.[12] Ducpétiaux was also well aware of the relation between working conditions and international competitiveness. In his book, *De la condition physique et morale des jeunes ouvriers et des moyens de l'améliorer*, published in 1843, he wrote:

> What argument is so often levelled against projects for industrial reform? It is the tyranny of competition. . . Man disappears in this desperate struggle; he is no longer anything more than a weapon with the aid of which blows are given or parried.
>
> . . .
>
> Let nations unite for social reform instead of frustrating one another's efforts. Let them summon a general congress to regulate their mutual concerns: commercial and industrial relations and the problems of the workers. All civilized nations should concur in this truly holy alliance which should open to humanity a new area of well-being and universal satisfaction.[13]

Congresses and Associations

Ducpétiaux was also one of the men calling for the first International Congress of Benevolence that was held at Brussels in

1856. One person who attended this congress was the theologian Chrisoph Ulrich Hahn who raised the question of international labour legislation by bringing up a project where he quoted Legrand, as follows:

> An international labour law is the only possible solution to the great social problem of granting moral and material well-being to the working class without working a hardship upon the manufacturers and without fair competition between industries of different countries being transformed into a competition which cuts the throats of the workers.[14]

The working conditions that were emphasised in Hahn's project were child labour, the duration of the workday and the question of weekly rest for children and adult female workers. The congress at Brussels deferred Hahn's proposal until the congress at Frankfurt in 1857 where a resolution along the same lines as Hahn's proposal was passed, with the exception of the question of duration of the workday.[15]

During the second half of the nineteenth century the proposals for international labour legislation increased. This is not surprising if the events in the economic structure of the Western world are taken into consideration. The process of industrialisation spread from England to other countries in Europe, and to the United States and Japan. The accompanying increases in international trade brought different countries closer together. Thereby, the fear of the presumed conflict between nationalistic policies in the field of labour legislation and international competitiveness become even more pronounced.

In the 1860s, the International Workingmen's Association was formed. Karl Marx drew up its Provisional Rules, based on considerations concerning the emancipation of the working class. With regard to international aspects:

> The emancipation of labour is neither a local nor a national, but a social problem embracing all countries in which modern society exists, and depending for its solution on the concurrence, practical and theoretical, of the most advanced countries.[16]

At the congress held by the Association in Geneva in 1866,

resolutions on hours of work and child labour were adopted. The maximum number of hours of work for adults were set at eight hours a day. With regard to child labour, the resolution set nine years of age as the minimum age for taking part in productive work. Between nine and 18 years of age, the number of hours that children should be allowed to work increased with the age, from two up to six hours a day. Furthermore, according to the resolutions of the congress, dangerous work and night work by women and children should be abolished.[17]

In the 1870s and the 1880s work continued on obtaining improvements of working conditions without at the same time reducing international competitiveness.[18] At a congress of academic socialists held in Eisenach in 1872, a paper was presented by Professor Bretano of the University of Breslau. His basic standpoint was that international labour legislation was unnecessary since he believed that improved working conditions would increase rather than reduce a nation's international competitiveness. Nevertheless, Bretano was clearly aware of how the relation between working conditions and competition in the world market could give rise to protectionism based on what he classified as 'short-sighted greed':

> The German free traders, by opposing such treaties [international treaties on labour] and encouraging long hours for women and minors. . . hinder the universal acceptance of free-trade principles. In America, particularly, the establishment of a high tariff wall is a rebuke to the long working hours of women and young people in Europe and their consequences upon family and society. 'As long as we can', say the Americans, 'we will avoid the development of such conditions among us.' If industry requires protection, it is better that a country pay the costs of it out of its money bags than through the sacrifice of its women and children.[19]

Besides child labour and hours of work, other working conditions were also discussed in the early years. In 1876, an international congress of hygiene, held in Brussels, advanced the view that international labour legislation 'would be designed chiefly to achieve uniform rules of hygiene and labour conditions'.[20] At the Sixth International Congress of Hygiene held in Vienna in 1877, the subjects of hygiene at the work place and international conventions were also discussed. Among the conclusions arrived at by the congress was the following:

> When certain serious dangers can be remedied only by the prohibition of certain modes of exploitation (as for example, the use of arsenic and white phosphorus), the measures to be taken ought to be arranged, as far as possible, through international conventions.[21]

During the 1880s, the labour leaders in Europe worked on forming a new International since the First International, the International Workingmen's Association, had lost its international character in the mid-seventies. In 1889 they succeeded in creating the Second International, the purpose of which was to work for social reforms through national and international legislation in the labour market. It was also decided to proclaim the first day of May as a general labour holiday on which workers throughout the world should organise demonstrations, thereby manifesting their demands and solidarity.[22]

Parallel to the work on forming the Second International, work was underway in Switzerland to prepare an official international conference on working conditions. In 1889, invitations were sent out to 13 European states.[23] However, the conference never took place – when the German Kaiser William II ordered Prime Minister Bismarck to invite foreign governments to a conference in Berlin, the invitation from the Swiss government was withdrawn.

The Berlin Conference in March 1890 was a failure due to inadequate preparation and the wish to cover too broad a field of labour questions.[24] However, even though the opponents of such legislation were pleased by this failure, it did not stop work on international labour legislation.

In 1897, the First International Congress on Labour Protection took place in Zurich.[25] Nearly 400 delegates represented organisations of workers in 14 countries. A resolution was passed in which the Swiss government was asked to invite other governments to set up a labour office.

In the same year, an important step was taken towards international labour legislation at a conference that took place in Brussels.[26] The delegates attending this conference were not trade union leaders but professors, economists and politicians. The purpose of the conference was not to pass any resolutions, but to discuss a set of questions such as the development of labour legislation in the different countries since the Berlin Conference; the possibilities and the desirability of international labour protection; and the question of establishing international exchange and compilation of labour statistics. In order to continue the work on these questions a committee was set up to 'seek means of giving effect to the congress'.[27] The members of this committee agreed that the aim of their work was to set up an international association for labour protection. In 1900, the statutes of the International Association for Labour Legislation were adopted in Paris. In 1901, the constitutive assembly of the Association decided to set up an International Labour Office in Basle. The office was opened on May Day 1901.[28]

Contrary to the Berlin Conference, the Association restricted its interest to the type of labour legislation that could be expected to meet least opposition. The first two subjects selected were the prohibition of the use of white phosphorus in industry and the prohibition of night work by women. Conferences dealing with these two subjects took place at Berne in 1905 and 1906. According to Mahaim 'the discussions which took place at Berne in 1905 and 1906 showed how acute was the opposition between country and country when questions of industrial competition were at stake'.[29]

The objects of the conventions were to equalise costs of production and standardise legislation. At the time of the conference Austria, France, Germany, Great Britain, Italy, the Netherlands and Switzerland already had prohibited night work by women. Other countries that signed the Night Work Convention at Berne were given up to twelve years to change their legislation.[30]

The convention on white phosphorus turned out to be more problematic. In 1905, this convention met strong opposition from countries with match industries where white phosphorus was an important input. In 1906, several countries were prepared to agree upon the convention only if Japan and British India prohibited the use of white phosphorus.[31] However, Denmark, Germany, the Netherlands, Switzerland, France, Luxemburg and Italy all agreed on the convention. Of these countries all but Luxemburg and Italy had already prohibited the use of white phosphorus by national legislation.

Many countries that did not agree on the convention at the Berne Conference soon prohibited the use of white phosphorus, due largely to the considerable number of cases of phosphorus necrosis. In fact, Sweden and Japan were the only major match exporting countries that in 1919 had not prohibited the use of white phosphorus.[32]

A new conference on labour legislation took place at Berne in 1913.[33] At that conference, the bases for two more conventions were worked out. One convention aimed at maximising hours of work to 60 hours a week for men below 16 years of age and all women. The other convention related to the prohibition of night work for all persons below 14 years of age and most persons below 16. These two conventions were to be formally signed at a diplomatic conference in September 1914. An invitation to the conference was also sent out by the Swiss government. However, the First World War broke out before the conference could take place.

Early Bilateral Agreements

Besides the importance of the Berne conventions on night work by women and the prohibition of the use of white phosphorus, we should also note the great number of bilateral agreements that were negotiated at the beginning of the twentieth century.[34] The first of these was the Franco-Italian Treaty of 1904. This treaty consisted of two parts; one dealt with the general conditions of labour, forcing Italy to regulate working conditions more in line with the conditions that already existed in France, while the other part gave Italian workers in France the same treatment as domestic workers in the case of industrial accidents and old age pensions and also gave young Italians working in France special protection. It is of historical interest to note that the first part of this treaty puts one of the contracting parties, Italy, in a less competitive position. Consequently, it is not surprising that the treaties that were agreed upon after the Franco-Italian Treaty of 1904 concentrated on the second part of the treaty. In 1914 no less than 28 bilateral agreements had been concluded, most of them giving migrant workers the same social security as domestic workers.[35]

The Treaty of Peace and the International Labour Organisation

During the war, the work on calling for a world labour conference continued in the United States as well as in Western Europe. Much of the work aimed at obtaining clauses on labour protection within the Treaty of Peace after the end of the war and establishing a permanent international labour office. Studying the preparatory work of the Peace Conference that took place in different countries, the central position of the relation between international competition and international labour standards is striking.[36] One example is given in the opening speech of the Committee on International Labour Treaties in France in 1917 where the chairman stressed the importance of international agreements:

> In questions such as hours of work, the regulation of dangerous trades, the prohibition of certain work for women and children, international competition may for a long time favor those countries which do not accept the highest standards of human conditions, to the serious detriment of more generous nations.[37]

Another example is taken from the British preparatory work where, in a memorandum on the results of discussions between the members of the labour section of the British delegation at the Peace Conference, one can read:

> Any State, therefore, which does not carry out a Convention designed to prevent oppressive conditions is guilty of manufacturing under conditions which create a state of unfair competition in the international market. The appropriate penalty accordingly appears to be that when a two-thirds majority of the Conference is satisfied that the terms of the Convention have not been carried out the signatory States should discriminate against the articles produced under the conditions of unfair competition proved to exist unless those conditions were remedied within one year or such longer period as the Conference might decide.[38]

Without going into a description of the work on international labour legislation at the Peace Conference, we can now turn to the resulting Constitution of the International Labour Organisation, which is Part XIII of the Treaty of Versailles.[39] It is outside the scope of this study to go into details regarding the different parts of this Constitution.[40] However, some remarks will be made. First, we notice that the International Labour Organisation (ILO), which was established by the approval of the Constitution, should be under the control of a governing body consisting of representatives of governments, employers and workers.[41] Furthermore, we notice that prominence is given to the relationship between labour standards and international competition. In the Preamble of the Constitution it is stated:

> Whereas also the failure of any nation to adopt human conditions of labour is an obstacle in the way of other nations which desire to improve the conditions in their own countries . . .[42]

Among the methods and principles of this organisation we read that special importance should be given to the following:

> *First.* – The guiding principle above enunciated that labour should not be regarded merely as a commodity or article of commerce.
> *Second.* – The right of association for all lawful purposes by the employed as well as by the employers.
> *Third.* – The payment to the employed of a wage adequate to maintain a reasonable standard of life as this is understood in their time and country.
> *Fourth.* – The adoption of an eight-hours day or a forty-eight-hours week as the standard to be aimed at where it has not already been attained.
> *Fifth.* – The adoption of a weekly rest of at least twenty-four hours, which should include Sunday wherever practicable.
> *Sixth.* – The abolition of child labour and the imposition of such limitations on the labour of young persons as shall permit the continuation of their education and assure their proper physical development.
> *Seventh.* – The principle that men and women should receive equal remuneration for work of equal value.
> *Eighth.* – The standard set by law in each country with respect to the conditions of labour should have due regard to the equitable economic treatment of all workers lawfully resident therein.
> *Ninth.* – Each State should make provision for a system of

> inspection in which women should take part, in order to ensure the enforcement of the laws and regulations for the protection of the employed.[43]

It should also be noted that there is a sort of reservation with regard to the possibilities of individual countries satisfying these requirements. The High Contracting Parties

> recognise that differences of climate, habits and customs, of economic opportunity and industrial tradition, make strict uniformity in the conditions of labour difficult of immediate attainment.[44]

Furthermore, we should notice that the ILO does not include any explicit trade policy sanctions for countries that do not satisfy the conditions expressed in conventions that have been adopted. However, the constitution of the organisation does not leave the question of sanctions aside. A member of the ILO has always the right to complain if it is of the opinion that another member does not satisfy conventions that both have ratified.[45] The governing body of the ILO may then take various actions to solve the problems referred to in the complaint. One such action is to leave the question to a commission of enquiry. This commission should investigate the basis of the complaint and make a report to the governing body. This report shall include a description of the economic measures that the commission considers appropriate and fair for other countries to adopt in their relations with the faulty member.

The report of the commission of enquiry should be distributed to the governments concerned who have to 'inform the Secretary General of the League of Nations whether or not it accepts the recommendations contained in the report'.[46] If a government does not accept the recommendations it has the right to refer the complaint to the Permanent Court of International Justice of the League of Nations, whose decision shall be final. Furthermore, the Constitution of the ILO states:

> In the event of any Member failing to carry out within the time specified the recommendations, if any, contained in the report of the Commission of Enquiry, or in the decision of the Permanent Court of International Justice, as the case may be,

> any other Member may take against that Member the measures of an economic character indicated in the report of the Commission or in the decision of the Court as appropriate to the case.[47]

In relation to the presentation of the possibilities of sanctions stated in the Constitution of the ILO, it should be noted that up to August 1981 only four cases have been referred to a commission of enquiry.[48] Nevertheless, the question of labour standards in trade policy has continued to be under debate. In the US Tariff Act of 1930, such standards were emphasised as a means of ensuring that international trade really gives rise to improved working and living standards. In fact the importation of commodities produced by means of 'convict labour or/and forced labour or/and indentured labour under penal sanctions' was prohibited by this act.[49] The argument of unfair competition based on exploited labour in foreign countries was also emphasised in the US debate on entering the ILO in the early 1930s.[50]

Labour Standards and Trade after the Second World War

After the Second World War, the question of labour standards and trade was reflected in the 1948 statutes of the International Trade Organisation (ITO):

> The Members recognize that . . . all countries have a common interest in the achievement and maintenance of fair labour standards related to productivity, and thus in the improvement of wages and working conditions as productivity may permit. The Members recognize that unfair labour conditions, particularly in production for export, create difficulties in international trade, and accordingly, each Member shall take whatever action may be appropriate and feasible to eliminate such conditions within its territory.[51]

However, the statutes of the ITO were never ratified. Instead the General Agreement on Tariffs and Trade (GATT), that was agreed upon in Geneva in 1947 as a part of the discussions on forming the ITO, became the organisation that would govern the liberalisation of international trade in the post-war period.

In GATT, we can find one article on labour standards – article

XX states that import restrictions may be applied against imports of products produced by prison labour. However, in a way we may say that GATT explicitly includes the labour standard article of ITO, as GATT article XXIX states that

> The contracting parties undertake to observe to the fullest extent of their executive authority the general principles of Chapters I to VI inclusive and of Chapter IX of the Havana Charter . . .

In the 1950s, the economic co-operation between European countries was intensified by the formation of the EEC and EFTA. In order to analyse the social aspects of this increase in co-operation and particularly the accompanying trade liberalisation, in 1955 the ILO appointed a group of experts, with Professor Bertil Ohlin acting as chairman.[52] One of the main questions analysed by this group related to the general need for social harmonisation coupled with the trade liberalisation connected with intensified European economic co-operation. In the group's report, presented in 1956, it was concluded that there was no such need as long as the differences in competitiveness between different countries are based on differences in the general wage levels and not on differences in wage levels between different industries inside individual countries.[53] Moreover, in these latter cases the group recommended caution, even though it was admitted that a basis for demanding harmonisation inside the individual countries could clearly exist.[54] Furthermore, the group of experts concluded that

> Wages and labour conditions are moreover, in European countries, usually the outcome of collective bargaining, and there is widespread agreement that government interference with the freedom of collective bargaining, if it becomes necessary at all, should be kept to a minimum.[55]
>
> . . .
>
> An attempt to establish identical patterns of relative wage rates and labour conditions in different industries in each of a number of countries would certainly represent an unduly rigid approach.[56]

> . . .
>
> It may nevertheless be found desirable and possible to 'harmonise' to some extent action for the improvement of workers' living standards.[57]
>
> . . . if workers in a particular industry in some countries are weakly organised or for some other reason are unable to obtain wage increases in step with rising productivity, the improvement of labour standards in the same or competing industries abroad may also be hampered. In such circumstances it would be desirable to create conditions for effective collective bargaining or, failing that, machinery for the statutory fixing of minimum wages in those cases where labour bargaining is weak.[58]

Before the above study on social aspects of European economic co-operation got under way, work had begun in 1954 on a European Social Charter for members of the Council of Europe. In October 1961, the final text was signed by the member states of this organisation at a meeting in Turin. The European Social Charter is based heavily on the conventions and instruments adopted by the ILO. Therefore, we will not enter into any further description of this Charter.[59]

In 1960 there was a meeting in Paris where US and European trade union economists discussed the incorporation of fair labour standards in international trade policy. The proposal for such an incorporation came from the US trade union economists. They suggested that 'countries receiving concessions on given commodities under the General Agreement on Tariffs and Trade (GATT) be required to report annually on progress achieved in working conditions and living standards in the industries concerned'.[60]

However, there were no proposals for accompanying the incorporation of labour standards with sanctions. Stanley Ruttenberg of the American Federation of Labor, Congress of Industrial Organisations (AFL-CIO) suggested three alternative ways of giving new competitive economies access to the markets of old industrial countries without making too large an impact on the situation in these countries:

(1) Assure fair competition in world markets by regulating

labor standards in exporting countries whose standards now give them unfair competitive advantage.

(2) Make sure that low-wage exports do not curtail employment opportunities and/or depress wage standards in the corresponding industry of importing countries.

(3) Give workers in the export industries maximum compensation within the economic capabilities of the industries.[61]

Another of the US economists, Everett Kassalow, also made the comment that fair labour standards in trade could be a means to forestall the increased use of protective trade policy measures.[62]

The European delegates were less enthusiastic. They feared that the United States might use the fair labour standard argument as a protectionistic device against imports from Europe. Furthermore, they expressed preferences for economic aid and international trade union activities prior to the introduction of some concept of fair labour standards as a means of improving working and living conditions in less developed countries.[63] With respect to the problems arising from imports from low-wage countries, the Swedish representative Tord Ekström of the Confederation of Swedish Trade Unions (LO), argued that these problems 'could be met by adjustment measures within importing countries which support general full employment policies'.[64] As an example he referred to the Swedish policy in the textile industry.

During the 1970s, the question of labour standards and trade policy has been subject to discussion several times. One example is given by the following quotation:

> In the textile sector there are now a number of over-industrialized countries with practically no domestic market and an economy exclusively directed towards exports. This abnormal situation is explained by the combination of low wages and high productivity, deriving in particular from working conditions which are unacceptable by European standards. There is no social or economic reason why the EEC should accept this unfair competition.[65]

There have also been several demands for introducing labour standards into the rules governing international trade. One such demand has come from the International Metalworkers'

Federation.[66] The Swedish Confederation of Trade Unions and the Swedish Central Organisation of Salaried Employees (TCO) have supported this demand and have also tried to persuade the government to work for a social clause in GATT. The Nordic countries have also worked for changes in GATT article XIX in order that the intentions behind the demands for such a clause will be satisfied as far as possible.[67]

In the United States the proposals for labour standards in trade policy have continued in the 1970s. For instance, in 1977 the AFL-CIO adopted a resolution on a code of international labour standards that envisages:

> Such a code should recognize the human rights of workers in all lands for free association, for organization and pursuit of democratic collective bargaining, and for withholding their labor in unacceptable working conditions. It should set minimum standards of comparability for total compensation according to the different rates of productivity prevailing in each nation's industries, and provide for enforcement of those standards within each country or by the country of origin of multinational enterprises. For exporting industries, failure to meet such minimum standards should trigger counter-balancing restraints on the importation of the products of unfair foreign competition, and such mechanisms should be sanctioned insofar as possible by international agreement.[68]

Furthermore, in 1978 the Executive Council of the AFL-CIO declared that 'Fair Labor Standards criteria must be applied to the acceptance of imports into US markets to assure fair competition. Foreign producers should be required to meet minimum labor standards or face import quotas and other trade restrictions.'[69]

Recently, the International Confederation of Free Trade Unions (ICFTU) has also suggested the incorporation of a social clause in international trade relations. Reference is made here to the interdependence between international competition and social policy.

> If minimum labour and social standards are not widely observed internationally, any single nation making social progress will be penalised by a decline in trading competitiveness. A social clause in trade agreemens would aim at

> preventing this. The objective would be to insert into the GATT and other treaties specific clauses designed to encourage social progress in line with economic development by reference to international labour standards. Benefits available to contracting parties under these treaties should therefore be made conditional upon the observance of such standards.
>
> . . .
>
> A social clause should include provisions making it possible to prohibit trade in products produced under conditions and methods which endanger workers' lives.[70]

The Departments of Labour in the United States and Canada have also published memoranda on labour standards and trade policy. A US paper presented in 1978 states that the incorporation of labour standards in trade policy is not intended to restrict trade but to protect an open trade system in the world. It is clearly stated also that sanctions should be secondary to the prime goal of promoting compliance with international labour standards. However, it is admitted that

> Sanctions, cannot be deferred indefinitely. The possibility of ultimate recourse to sanctions, after an appropriate phase-in period of technical assistance, will assure workers in developed countries imports are not based on flagrant exploitation of workers.[71]

In October 1979, the United States continued the work in this field by making a submission to GATT proposing minimum international labour standards as a means of satisfying the objective contained in the GATT Preamble relating to 'raising standards of living'.

> The objective of such labor standards would be to deal with: (a) differential standards favoring export sectors within a given country, and (b) certain working conditions which are dangerous to life and health at any level of development. The imposition of uniform labor standards on all trading nations would not be the purpose.[72]

In a 1979 Canadian memorandum the solidarity aspect of

incorporating labour standards in trade policy is further emphasised:

> A fair labour standards system would help those of the developing countries which are seeking to improve their labour standards but may be deterred by the threat of competition from countries which are less scrupulous.[73]

The same line of argument can be found in the EEC proposal on introducing labour standards in the Lomé Convention.[74] This proposal advances two aims to be gained from such an incorporation. First, developing countries with working conditions that satisfy international labour conventions should not be penalised in their trade with the EEC by being outcompeted by countries that do not comply with such conventions. Secondly, the incorporation of labour standards in the agreements would mean that the EEC supports a development policy with social aims. The conventions proposed for the agreement were the conventions on non-discrimination, hours of work and child labour. For future incorporation, conventions on minimum wages, freedom of association, organisation, collective bargaining and occupational safety and health were mentioned.

The relation between labour standards and trade policy was explicitly declared in this proposal which states that trade preferences given by the EEC to developing countries will require that working conditions in these developing countries satisfy the minimum requirements expressed in the incorporated labour standards. However, the proposal was rejected by the developing countries. Instead, the Economic and Social Committee of the EEC in 1980 adopted the following statement:

> In the Committee's view, compliance with labour standards should not be equated with protectionist rules or serve as a pretext for restrictive measures in the area of trade and cooperation in general. If protection is considered necessary, especially in trade matters, the case for it must be considered separately, and not in conjunction with the question of standards.[75]

However, further reading clarifies that labour standards and trade relations are still linked together in this document. On the question of such commercial relations as the Generalised System of Preferences (GSP), between industrialised countries and developing countries, we can read that 'the donors and beneficiaries of these advantages [e.g. the GSPs] should . . . jointly seek adequate ways of ensuring compliance by the States concerned with minimum social standards in accordance with ILO conventions'.[76]

We should also note that the question of labour standards and trade has been observed in the 1980 *Brandt Report*. Among the recommendations we find: 'Fair labour standards should be internationally agreed in order to prevent unfair competition and to facilitate trade liberalization.'[77]

Finally, it is worth noting that in a specific area of international trade, trade in primary products, there have recently been concluded agreements that in some cases include labour standards provisions. However, the manner in which the standards are incorporated in these agreements, is, as a rule, imprecise and not binding for the parties involved.[78]

Following this historical review of demands for an incorporation of labour standards in trade policy, we will now comment on the arguments that have been advanced against such an incorporation.

The Opposition Against an Incorporation of Labour Standards in Trade Policy – Some Comments

The arguments advanced in favour of an incorporation of labour standards in trade policy can be classified into three quite distinct categories: (a) protection of domestic working conditions and production; (b) solidarity with foreign workers; and (c) protection of an open international trade system. In a similar manner, the arguments against such an incorporation can be divided into different categories.[79]

First, there are the arguments concerned with the practical possibilities of incorporating labour standards in trade policy. One of these arguments maintains that it is impossible to have a uniform set of labour standards in different countries since climate, culture and the state of economic development differ among the countries of the world.[80] This problem was recognised and explicitly dealt with in the Constitution of the ILO. Another line of argument is to claim that a set of labour standards in the rules of international trade will be difficult to implement efficiently.[81]

Turning to the economic arguments that are advanced against an incorporation of labour standards in trade policy, the most important argument is of course that there is no general economic justification for it. Another closely related and frequently cited argument is that such an incorporation is motivated solely by protectionism.[82] Since, as a rule, the gains from trade are accepted as a convincing proposition, open deviation from the principle of free trade is resisted. However, even if labour standards are kept outside the rules that govern international trade, differences in working conditions among countries may well be significant as arguments in the demands for protectionism. This is also the argument put forward by those who consider that an incorporation of labour standards in trade policy can protect the international trade system against increased use of traditional trade barriers. However, to be a valid argument in favour of labour standards in trade policy, this type of policy must be proved to be superior to other types of trade policy.

Another argument against labour standards in trade policy is that developed countries, through the incorporation of labour standards in trade policy, seek to place the burden of their own economic problems on less developed countries.[83] Consequently, the possibilities of economic development will be hampered, especially for the latter group of countries. Once again, it is important to remember that working conditions in developing countries may also well be advanced as an argument for protectionism directed against imports from these countries when the rules that govern international trade do not include labour standards. Therefore, it is important to investigate how different trade policy measures affect the countries that face increased protectionism in their export markets.

A political argument of significant weight against an incorporation of labour standards in trade policy is that such an incorporation will imply severe interference with the domestic conditions of sovereign countries.[84] This argument is always very important when consideration is given to the practical possibilities of reaching international agreements that imply significant deviations from the present situation or policy of individual countries. As has been noted above, in the Preamble of the ILO, and also in more recent documents on labour standards in trade policy, this argument has been used for the opposite purpose. When international trade increases, the possibilities of sovereign policy formation are reduced for individual countries. Consequently, there is a demand for harmonisation. As already mentioned, a group of experts, chaired by Professor Ohlin, found that, as a rule, there was no general need for harmonisation of labour standards when the European countries increased their interdependence by the formation of the EEC and EFTA. However, in the absence of trade unions and collective bargaining, the Ohlin group admitted that demands for harmonisation could be motivated.

From the above, we can conclude that besides political and practical arguments against an incorporation of labour standards in trade policy, economic arguments have been advanced based upon a fear of increased protectionism and its consequences, especially for the less developed countries of the world. As an absence of labour standards in trade policy does not mean that differences in working conditions do not provide a basis for introducing trade barriers against exports from developing countries, it is important to investigate the differences of the effects of different types of trade policies, including a policy where labour standards are explicitly incorporated. This will also be one of the aims of this study, but before we proceed with the analysis we will briefly describe the recent development of trade policy as well as considering the political economy of protectionism in order to put the present study into an empirical trade policy context.

Summary

The question of international labour standards and trade is of longstanding importance. The awareness of the relation between working conditions and international competitiveness was one of the main forces behind the century-long work involved in forming an international organisation on labour questions. This work resulted in the formation of the ILO in 1919. Thereafter, much of the work has taken place inside this organisation. However, besides this work there have been several demands and proposals for a close connection between labour standards and trade policy, a connection that does not exist within the constitution of the ILO. Labour standards that have been advanced as important for an incorporation are:

- freedom of association and the right to organise and

collective bargaining
- wages
- hours of work
- child labour
- occupational health and safety
- forced labour
- labour market discrimination

The aims of incorporating labour standards in the rules that govern international trade, as advanced by its advocates, are to improve the situation of foreign workers working under 'poor' working conditions and to protect the international trade system against increased protectionism. The opponents, on the other hand, have argued that the aim of such an incorporation is purely protectionistic. Furthermore, it is argued, such an incorporation would be difficult to implement efficiently and would also mean a severe interference with the domestic conditions of sovereign states.

1.2 Free Trade or Protectionism?

Recent Trade Policy

Without any doubt, the period after the Second World War can be characterised as a period of trade liberalisation. The formation of the General Agreement on Tariffs and Trade (GATT) in Geneva 1947 paved the way for this liberalisation. Regional trade in Western Europe was further liberalised by the formation of the EEC and EFTA in the 1950s. However, it should be noted that post-war trade liberalisation has merely been a liberalisation of the trade between the industrialised market economies while the liberalisation of the trade between developed and developing countries has been less far-reaching. Besides the formation of the EEC and EFTA, this can be explained by the composition of trade and the principle of reciprocity of GATT.

As long as the expansion in trade is dominated by intra-industry trade, problems of structural adjustment in the trading economies are less difficult to handle since the adjustment in this case can take place inside the individual sectors of the economy. In the case of increased inter-industry trade the structural adjustment has to take place not inside but between the different sectors of the economy. The trade expansion of the 1950s and 1960s was dominated by intra-industry trade and the trading economies experienced a steady economic growth. Therefore, it is not surprising to find that international trade in manufactures, with the exception of trade in textiles and clothing, was relatively free in the early 1970s.[85] However, in the first half of the seventies there was a clear break in the trend of economic growth as well as in the trend of trade liberalisation. One important explanation of this is the failure to handle the problems that arose in connection with the oil crisis in 1973 and 1974.[86] From October 1973 until January 1974 the oil-exporting countries in OPEC raised the price of oil by around 300 per cent. A direct consequence of this was increased savings in the oil-exporting countries which were unable to carry out investments of that magnitude. Neither were there any transfers of the savings which would have allowed a corresponding increase in investments outside OPEC. Another direct consequence was that the oil-importing countries suffered difficulties with their balance of payments. The belief that the producer cartel in the oil market would break after a few months led the political authorities in the industrial world to contract their economies. However, this view of the lifetime of the cartel and the high prices soon turned out to be wrong. Furthermore, the problem of excess saving in the oil-exporting economies was not successfully dealt with. Instead, there was a continuation of contractive economic policies. This sequence of political activities led to a deep recession and very high unemployment figures in OECD.

Besides the recession, many countries in the old industrial world also witnessed structural problems due to the entry of increased competition in the international market for industrial goods. Much of this increased competition came from new industrial countries which began to take advantages of their abundance of cheap labour. The accompanying increased exports of labour-intensive manufactures from these countries placed many domestic firms in the old industrial world in a very weak position. We should also note that the expansion in trade between developed and developing countries was dominated by inter-industry trade. In times of recession, problems connected with the process of structural adjustment, especially when the latter is induced by increased inter-industry trade, are difficult to handle since there is a weaker rate of growth in the expansive parts of the economy.

One consequence of the increased problems of structural adjustment in the old industrial world in the years after the oil crisis was a rise in protectionism.[87] To give an exact measure of the magnitude of this rise is very difficult since much of the trade policy has been designed in a way that conceals it from detection. One approximation that has been made by GATT is that some 3–5 per cent of the total world trade was affected by the protective measures adopted by developed market economies during the three years between 1974 and 1977.[88] It should be noted that this figure does not include trade policy measures that had been implemented before 1974 and that were still restricting trade during the period in question. Consequently, trade in textiles and clothing, approximately some five per cent of world trade, is not included since this trade has been restricted heavily since the early 1960s.[89] If we look closer at the available information on the protectionism of the 1970s, we notice that the trade restrictions have been mainly directed against Japan and the less developed countries.[90]

As is well known from both theory and experiences of the 1950s and 1960s there are great gains to be derived from keeping trade free. Furthermore, it should be noted that the economic problems that underlie demands for trade barriers, e.g. balance of payment problems and problems of structural adjustment and unemployment, can be dealt with more efficiently by using other policy measures than those of trade policy. A change in the rate of exchange can be used to reduce balance of payment problems. Furthermore, tax-cum-subsidy programmes can be constructed that are more efficient than various trade policy measures, e.g. tariffs and quotas, in dealing with problems of structural adjustment and unemployment.[91]

Why then can the advocates of protectionism succeed in making politicians enforce trade barriers? To give some possible answers to this question we now turn to the field of political economy.

The Political Economy of Protectionism

In the basic theory of international trade we learn that free trade, as a rule, gives rise to the highest potential welfare for an economy. From this, it is often concluded that a free trade policy is always the optimal policy. However, it is important to keep in mind that a change in trade policy towards a more liberal international trade does not by itself imply increased social welfare in the sense of the Pareto criteria. Policy actions have to be taken in the field of income distribution in order to guarantee such an improvement. The liberalisation of trade has an effect on income distribution. In general, factors that are used intensively in the import-competing sector of the economy will lose and have to be compensated in order to achieve an improvement in welfare. On the other hand, other groups, viz. other factors of production and consumers, will be made better off when the prices of import-competing commodities are reduced through trade liberalisation. Of course, the same line of argument is valid when import-competing industries face increased competition from foreign producers due to changes in comparative advantages under a given trade policy regime. If no trade barriers are set up to limit the effects of the increased foreign competitiveness, some factors of production will lose while other groups will gain. As trade policy actions are the result of political actions, it may be worthwhile to take a closer look at the factors that determine these activities in order to improve the possibilities of understanding and predicting trade policy formation.

Starting with the case where direct referendums determine the set of policy actions, reference is often made to the Stolper-Samuelson theorem to explain the measures taken to protect labour-intensive industries from increased import competition.[92] However, it should be remembered that the Stolper-Samuelson theorem deals with long run changes since it takes total re-allocation effects into account. For policy considerations it would seem realistic to assume that short run effects will dominate the long run effects, since the lack of information increases very rapidly over time. By definition, in the short run some factors of production are assumed to be sector specific. If all factors but labour are immobile between the different sectors of production, other factors that are also used in the industry facing the increased import competition, will gain from protectionism in the short run. With regard to the short run attitude of the workers, the degree of substitutability and the relative weights of non-protected and protected commodities in their consumption budgets will be decisive. In the short run, there will clearly be a greater chance of labour supporting a protectionistic policy when the protected commodity only makes up a minor part of the workers' total consumption or when the degree of substitutability is high between protected and non-protected commodities.

Consequently, in such cases the number of votes for protectionistic policy actions against labour-intensive imports will be larger when the short run considerations dominate the long run considerations.

Following the old argument of free trade, that everybody can be made better off by trade liberalisation, one natural question is why those directly favoured by the liberalisation do not compensate the losers from such a policy so that they give up their votes for protectionism. According to Baldwin such compensation schemes do exist in most countries but do not fully compensate the injured parties.[93] One underlying reason is that a compensatory scheme requires a costly administration for determining who are to be compensated as well as how much compensation each injured party should receive.

Another reason, mentioned by Baldwin, is that income compensation schemes may worsen the adjustment problems in the importing economy. Reference is made to the special unemployment benefits to trade-displaced workers in the United States: 'there is evidence suggesting that . . . [these unemployment benefits] may make employers more willing to lay off workers and encourage those who do lose their jobs to remain unemployed for longer periods than otherwise'.[94] Furthermore, uncertainty exists about the size of the burden that different groups in society would have to bear under a compensation scheme while this uncertainty does not exist under regimes of restricted trade, where the burden is distributed by the price system. The implication of this is that risk-averse voters would prefer restricted trade to a free trade regime combined with a compensation scheme.

Baldwin also refers to an empirical phenomenon concerning the financing of compensatory schemes that can increase the votes against free trade. The phenomenon in mind is that such schemes as well as other income subsidies may be financed through a progressive income tax system. The choice between free trade, including income subsidies to injured individuals, and restricted trade may well lead the voters with high incomes to vote for restricted trade rather than face lower prices that are made possible by free trade and increased taxes.

In the political debate, protectionistic arguments are often based heavily on the pure self-interest type of argument that underlies much of the results derived in economic theory. If the traditional individual utility functions are extended to include altruistic preferences as well, for instance so that the welfare of one individual depends positively on the welfare of other individuals, the sympathy for individuals injured by increased import competition can make voters vote for a trade-restricting policy even if they, from a pure self-interest point of view, would be expected to support a free trade policy.[95] Of special interest for the demands for labour standards in trade policy and the protection of industries that face increased foreign competition based on what is thought of as 'unfair' working conditions, is the 'generalized regard for human rights, social codes, business "ethics" and so on'.[96]

However, we should not forget that an individual, in supporting a trade-restrictive policy that protects other individuals from unemployment, may hope to increase the likelihood of other individuals supporting such policy measures in cases where the individual's own employment is threatened by foreign competition.

The problem of information has already been mentioned among the arguments that can explain why free trade compensatory schemes can be rejected if a referendum is used in determining trade policy. Since the costs of protection are distributed among all consumers of the protected good the cost falling on an individual consumer is so small that, as a rule, it is not worthwhile for him to collect information on the true costs that the policy gives rise to, nor to work actively for a more liberal trade policy by voting or otherwise.

If we leave the case of direct democracy and turn to the case of indirect democracy where policies are determined by political parties, the costs connected with active political work against trade restrictions will obviously increase. Under such a system, imperfections often exist that function as barriers of entry for new political parties to enter real politics. Of course the existence of imperfections in the political market implies a risk that public opinion is not always reflected in political decisions. In this case, each existing political party is assumed to choose the trade policy programme that maximises the possibilities for election.[97] Thereby the parties become easily influenced by different pressure groups. Since protectionistic policy can be characterised as a public good, in the sense that all firms and workers in the protected industry receive protection independently of their activities in lobbying, there is a clear free rider problem. According to Olson, pressure groups tend to arise if the group advocating the policy is small and if the benefits from the policy are unevenly distributed in the economy.[98] According to Pincus, pressure groups or lobbying will be more frequent if the interest group is geographically concentrated.[99] The reason is that under such circumstances, the costs connected with exercising the pressure will be lower than otherwise. This may explain why geographically concentrated and relatively small industries may succeed in obtaining protection even though it is unfavourable to the large number of geographically dispersed consumers.

Summary

After a period of trade liberalisation in the 1950s and 1960s, there has been an increased reliance on protectionistic measures in the 1970s, especially with regard to manufacturing exports from Japan and less developed countries. This break in the post-war trend of trade liberalisation has taken place notwithstanding the general awareness of the gains from international trade.

By looking at the political economy of protectionism, we can conclude that there are many arguments that point to great difficulties in avoiding protectionism in the future, especially in times of recession and when the growth in trade is dominated by inter-industry trade. However, this conclusion should not lead economists to give up the struggle for a more liberal trade system. Indeed, it is most important that economists place strong emphasis on the need for less frequent trade restrictions and point to more efficient policy measures for dealing with economic problems. On the other hand, it should not prevent us from analysing the effects of different types of trade policy regimes. In fact, the pessimism regarding the possibilities of free trade should make us anxious to analyse various trade policy measures in order that the least harmful measures are chosen, given the aims of the policy.

1.3 The Aim and Plan of the Study

In the previous sections, we have described the background of this study. We have noticed that both the labour standard argument for trade restrictions and the struggle for international legislation on working conditions have been with us for some considerable time. Notwithstanding the formation of the ILO more than 60 years ago, the demands for incorporating labour standards in trade policy still appear. As already noted the Ohlin report on social aspects of European economic co-operation dealt with the question of whether social harmonisation between countries is needed or motivated when international trade is liberalised. The answer given in that report was that as a general rule this is not the case. Nevertheless, during the last decade the demands for incorporating labour standards in trade policy have been frequent and so has the use of protectionistic policy measures, especially against imports from countries that are said to base their competitiveness on 'unfair' working conditions. With this background in mind and considering the explanations for the use of protectionistic means, an analysis, not so much of the economic justification but of the economic effects of an explicit incorporation of labour standards or social clauses in trade policy, seems to be highly warranted.[100] The overall aim of the present study is to carry out such an analysis.

As a reference point for the analysis, we will use the three groups of motives or aims that have been advanced in the debate concerning the incorporation of labour standards or social clauses in the rules that govern international trade. These aims are to

- provide protection to domestic industries and workers in the 'old' industrial countries;
- represent an action of solidarity with workers that now are working under 'unacceptably low' working conditions; and
- protect the international 'free trade system' from increased protectionism based on traditional trade barriers.

In Chapter 2, we analyse the economic aspects of a social clause on basic trade union rights, whereas Chapter 3 is devoted to an economic analysis of clauses on specific working conditions, namely wages, hours of work, child labour and occupational health and safety. In connection with the analysis in both these chapters, we will also give some brief information on the current situation with regard to working conditions in the newly industrialised countries in Latin America and South-east Asia that have made great progress as producers and exporters of manufactures during the last decades.

Due to the difficulties in specifying the economic characteristics of basic trade union rights, the analysis in Chapter 2 is limited to the relationship between such rights on the one hand, and economic development and economic welfare on the other. The labour standards analysed in Chapter 3 are more precise and thereby also more amenable to an economic interpretation. Therefore, the effects of social clauses on such standards are more straightforward to analyse.

To determine the effects on such factors as production, national income, employment and income distribution, in Chapter 3 we use a general equilibrium model where the short run as well as the long run effects of an introduction of social clauses on different specific working conditions are analysed. The general equilibrium analysis in Chapter 3 differs in three ways from the traditional analysis. First, our model will describe an economy consisting of three and not, as traditionally assumed, two sectors of production. However, due to the way the third sector is incorporated this difference is of minor importance from a theoretical point of view. The motive for our modelling is mainly to be found in reality as will be made clear in Chapter 3. The second difference is that the analysis deals with two types of economies with different labour market characteristics. In traditional general equilibrium analyses, full capacity utilisation, including full employment, is assumed. In our analysis besides *full employment economies*, economies characterised by unemployment will also be analysed. These types of economies will be called *labour surplus economies*. Finally, the third way in which our analysis differs from traditional analysis is through the time perspective. Traditionally, only long run effects are analysed, whereas we divide our analysis of the long run effects into two parts; one is devoted to the short run effects while the other deals with the economy's adjustment to a new long run equilibrium.

The analysis in Chapter 3 is based on the assumption of free trade in absence of the analysed social clauses. However, we know that the existence of defective working conditions can give rise to demands for trade barriers against imports of products produced under such conditions, even without social clauses. Furthermore, in section 1.2 we have noted that world trade today is restricted by many different trade barriers and that there is an obvious risk for increased protectionism, especially in times of recession and if less developed countries continue to make fast progress in their production and export penetration of labour-intensive manufactures. The advocates of social clauses claim that one of the aims of inserting such clauses into the rules governing international trade is to protect the trade system from increased protectionism based on traditional policy measures. An argument of this kind implies that social clauses would be superior to traditional protectionistic means. With this argument and the current empirical situation in mind, a comparison of the economic effects of social clauses with the effects of traditional trade policy measures would seem to be necessary in an analysis of the economic effects of incorporating social clauses in trade policy. In Chapter 4 we carry out a comparative analysis of this type. In conformity with earlier analyses of equivalences and non-equivalences between tariffs, import quotas and voluntary export restraints, we try to identify, in our analysis, similarities and differences between social clauses and other more traditional trade policy measures.

Our comparative study differs in three ways from the previous studies. First, the earlier studies analyse the effects on the importing countries which impose trade barriers, while our study also analyses the effects on the exporting countries affected by the different barriers. Secondly, the previous studies are mainly concentrated on the effects on prices, while our analysis of the effects on the exporting economies hit by the trade policies also takes into account the effects on national income, employment and income distribution. Finally, the earlier studies deal with non-discriminatory trade policy measures whereas this study compares different discriminatory measures.

The economic analysis of an enforcement of different social clauses is based on an assumption that the actual clauses are given a precise form and that the enforcement is effective in the sense that the actual clause really can be used in practical trade policy. Therefore, in Chapter 5, where we analyse the policy implications of the analysis and the relation between social clauses and the present rules governing international trade, GATT, we also make some comments on the practical problems of making social clauses operative and efficient.

To summarise. In the present study we will analyse the following questions:

- What is the empirical support for different social clauses?

- What will the economic effects be on economies hit by the different social clauses?
- What are the equivalences and non-equivalences between different social clauses on the one hand and different forms of traditional protectionistic policy means on the other?

Finally, we will analyse the policy implications of our analysis and relate the findings to the existing General Agreement on Tariffs and Trade.

Notes

1. See e.g. Baumol (1971), Johnson *et al.* (1968), ILO (1956), GATT (1971) and Robson (1980), and references therein.
2. The main sources for the description of the history of 'international labour legislation and trade' up to 1920 have been Shotwell (1934), US Department of Labor (1920), Solano (1920), Mahaim (1934) and Follows (1951).
3. Owen (1858), pp 207–22.
4. See Follows (1951), Ch. 1, Mahaim (1934), p. 4 and Krawtschenko (1910). See also the two Memorials by Owen (1858), pp. 207–22.
5. Follows (1951), p. 10.
6. Ibid.
7. J.A. Blanqui, *Cours d'economie industrielle, 1838–1839* (Paris 1839), here quoted from Mahaim (1934), p. 4.
8. Follows (1951), p. 67.
9. Mahaim (1934), p. 4.
10. ILO (1978), p. 3.
11. D. Legrand. *Appel respectueux adressé aux gouvernements des Pays Industrielles,. . .* (Strasbourg, 1855), here quoted from Follows (1951), p. 38.
12. Follows (1951), p. 43.
13. Here quoted from Follows (1951), pp. 45, 46.
14. *Congrès international de bienfaisance de Bruxelles – Session de 1856* (Brussels, 1957), here quoted from Follows (1951), p. 53.
15. Follows (1951), p. 57.
16. Ibid., p. 60.
17. Ibid., p. 61.
18. See Follows (1951), Chs. VIII–XI for a description of this work.
19. *Verhandlungen der Eisenacher Versammlung zur Besprechung der Sozialen Frage* (Leipzig, 1873), here quoted from Follows (1951), p. 82. See also US Department of Labor (1920), p. 29.
20. L. Combe, *De la legislation internationale du travail* (Paris, 1897), here quoted from Follows (1951), p. 107.
21. *VI. Internationaler Kongress für Hygiene und Demographie zu Wien 1887* (Vienna, 1887), quoted from Follows (1951), pp. 108, 109.
22. US Department of Labor (1920), pp. 50f.
23. Follows (1951), p. 121.
24. Ibid., pp. 132–43; see also US Department of Labor (1920), pp. 116–18.
25. ILO (1978), p. 4.

26. Follows (1951), pp. 151, 152; see also US Department of Labor (1920), p. 84.
27. Follows (1951), p. 152.
28. Ibid., p. 156; see also US Department of Labor (1920), p. 89.
29. Mahaim (1934), p. 9.
30. Ibid., p. 10; see also US Department of Labor (1920), pp. 128–32. The text of the convention can be found in Follows (1951), Appendix VI.
31. Follows (1951), p. 163; see also US Department of Labor (1920), pp. 132–3.
32. Follows (1951), p. 167.
33. Ibid., pp. 174, 175; see also US Department of Labor (1920), pp. 134–7.
34. Ibid., pp. 170, 171; see also US Department of Labor (1920), pp. 138–62 for a description of the treaties.
35. For a description of the recent development concerning the number and content of bilateral trèaties, see e.g. Valticos (1979), pp. 67f and references therein.
36. Shotwell (1934), Ch. IV.
37. Picquenard (1934), p. 86.
38. Phelan (1934), p. 118.
39. For a detailed description, see Shotwell (1934), pp. 424f.
40. Ibid., see also ILO (1980).
41. Shotwell (1934), p. 428.
42. Ibid., p. 425.
43. Ibid., pp. 448–50.
44. Ibid., p. 448.
45. Ibid., p. 438.
46. Ibid., pp. 441–2.
47. Ibid., p. 443.
48. Information received from ILO.
49. *US Tariff Act of 1930*, p. 112.
50. Lindsay (1934), pp. 362–7.
51. UN (1948), Article 7(1).
52. See ILO (1956).
53. Ibid., pp. 40f.
54. Ibid., p. 62.
55. Ibid.
56. Ibid.
57. Ibid., p. 88.
58. Ibid., pp. 88, 89.
59. See 'The European Social Charter and International Labour Standards' (1961).
60. Mintzes (1960), p. 1025.
61. Ibid., p. 1027.
62. Ibid., p. 1030.
63. Ibid., p. 1025.
64. Ibid., p. 1030.
65. European Parliament, *Bulletin 78/2* (Dec. 1977).
66. The International Metalworkers' Federation has demanded a social clause that as well as fair labour standards also includes employment guarantee, income guarantee, public control of social and economic readaptation and anticipatory structural adjustment measures. See *Proposal Concerning a Social Clause to be Inserted in the G.A.T.T. Treaty* (1976).
67. Utrikesutskottets betänkande 1978/79: 1, pp. 26–7.
68. US Department of Labor (1978), p. 7.

69. Ibid., p. 16.
70. ICFTU (1979), Appendix.
71. US Department of Labor (1978), p. 14.
72. *Proposal on Minimum International Labor Standards*, US submission to GATT (Oct. 1979).
73. Department of Labour, Canada (1979), p. 4.
74. *Udviklingssamarbejde og Overholdelse af visse Internationale Normer for Arbejdsvilkår* (1978).
75. EEC Economic and Social Committee (1980), opinion of p. 4.
76. Ibid., p. 12.
77. The Independent Commission on International Development Issues (1980), p. 186.
78. For a recent review and debate, see e.g. Alston (1981) and Kullman (1980).
79. A recent example of the debate on the subject is the debate between Säve-Söderbergh (1978a, b) and Hamilton (1978a, b).
80. See e.g. Sanger (1920).
81. Ibid., see also Hamilton (1978a, b).
82. See for instance any basic economics textbook for a discussion of the *cheap labour argument*. See also Hamilton (1978a, b).
83. Ibid.
84. Sanger (1920) and Hamilton (1978a, b).
85. See e.g. IMF (1978).
86. For a description and discussion of the 'oil crisis', see e.g. Södersten (1980), pp. 468f.
87. See e.g. Balassa (1978), Burenstam-Linder (1980), Gard and Riedel (1980), IMF (1978), Long (1977, 1978), Sampson (1980) and UNCTAD (1978).
88. UNCTAD (1978), p. 16.
89. Long (1978).
90. See e.g. IMF (1978).
91. See e.g. Bhagwati (1971).
92. Stolper and Samuelson (1941).
93. The following description relies heavily on Baldwin (1980), in which the studies and results of the 'political economy of protectionism' are efficiently summarised.
94. Ibid., p. 30.
95. See e.g. Phelps (1975), Arrow (1975).
96. Phelps (1975), p. 2.
97. Brock and Magee (1978).
98. Olson (1965).
99. Pincus (1975).
100. For an analysis of the relation between international labour legislation and economic theory see also Feis (1927).

2 A SOCIAL CLAUSE ON BASIC TRADE UNION RIGHTS

2.1 Introduction

In the Western industrialised world, as a rule, workers are relatively free to form and act through trade unions. Thereby they also have the opportunity to work collectively for improvements in various working conditions. As basic trade union rights can be assumed to be an essential requirement for the successful introduction of changes in specific working conditions that are in line with the preferences held by workers, it seems natural to start the analysis of social clauses by taking a closer look at a clause that deals with such rights.

Looking at history we find that the rise of trade unions is usually connected with the process of industrialisation. The higher level of mechanisation in production made it possible for unskilled workers to obtain industrial employment at better terms than was the case in other sectors of the economy. As a consequence, the number of workers searching for jobs in the industry increased, often at such a rate that a large excess supply of labour came into existence. At the local and regional level, the position of individual workers was very weak compared to the position of employers. This situation made it possible for employers to hire workers even though working conditions were very poor. The individual worker simply had to accept the conditions offered in order to get a job. To achieve more equal terms with employers, and thereby increase the possibility of obtaining better working conditions, the workers soon found that they had to act together. For this purpose they tried to form trade unions.

However, in the early days of industrialisation, the workers met strong opposition in their attempts to form unions.[1] In many countries, the legislation against workers' rights to organise suppressed the development of trade unions. This policy was often supported by economists who at that time, as well as today, were primarily concerned with wages and employment in their analysis of the labour market.[2] Working conditions, apart from the wage level, were not considered to any great extent. Opposition was strengthened by the fact that the workers, or at least their leaders, were often involved in political parties with socialist aims.

In the second half of the nineteenth century, the right of workers to organise began to be tolerated in North America and Western Europe. This was largely due to the strength of the labour movement, in the labour market as well as on the political scene, that had arisen notwithstanding the strong opposition and legislation against trade unions.[3] However, this public tolerance did not indicate an acceptance of workers' right to form and act through unions. On the contrary, in North America and several European countries there still existed laws that restricted the opportunity of workers to act together in trade unions.[4]

From the end of the nineteenth century the laws in the industrialised countries changed in favour of trade unions and in the first decades of the twentieth century the right to organise was explicitly established by law. When the International Labour Organisation was formed in 1919, emphasis was given to the rights of workers to form and act through trade unions. Today, basic trade union rights are commonly associated with the ILO conventions nos. 87 and 98 on the freedom of association and protection of the right to organise (no. 87) and the right of organisation and collective bargaining (no. 98).[5] According to these conventions,

> Workers and employers, without distinction whatsoever, shall have the right to establish and, subject only to the rules of the organisation concerned, to join organisations of their own choosing without previous authorisation.[6]
>
> Workers' and employers' organisations shall have the right to draw up their constitutions and rules, to elect their representatives in full freedom, to organise their administration and activities and to formulate their programmes.[7]
>
> The public authorities shall refrain from any interference which would restrict this right or impede the lawful exercise thereof.[8]
>
> . . .
>
> Workers' and employers' organisations shall have the right to establish and join federations and confederations and any such organisation, federation or confederation shall have the right to affiliate with international organisations of workers and employers.[9]

> . . .
>
> Workers shall enjoy adequate protection against acts of anti-union discrimination in respect of their employment.[10]
>
> . . .
>
> Measures appropriate to national conditions shall be taken, where necessary, to encourage and promote the full development and utilization of machinery for voluntary negotiation between employers or employers' organisations, with a view to the regulation of terms and conditions of employment by means of collective agreements.[11]

In July 1981, 93 countries had ratified ILO convention no. 87 and 115 countries had ratified convention no. 98.[12] Even though the rights demanded in these conventions are seen as a part of basic human rights in many countries, especially in the Western industrialised world, we could still find countries where these rights do not exist or only exist in a restricted sense.

In this chapter we will first present some indications of the present juridical situation regarding basic trade union rights in some of the newly industrialised countries (NICs) outside Europe, in order to exemplify some of the restrictive practices that apply to workers' legal rights to form and act through unions. We also discuss the problems of obtaining efficient trade unions in developing countries when basic trade union rights are legally protected.

The economic analysis of a social clause on basic trade union rights is far from a straightforward and easy task. Basic trade union rights may apply to a wide range of activities, of both an economic and non-economic nature. Since a social clause that deals with trade union rights cannot be expected to include any claims concerning the use of these rights, our attention will be focused upon two controversial issues that concern trade unions. The controversies, that have long been subjects of debate in economic literature, deal with the relationship between trade unions on the one hand and economic development and economic welfare on the other. In the literature, the negative influences of trade unions have received major attention. Therefore, in this chapter we will take a critical look at the assumptions and analyses that underlie the conclusions that trade unions tend to give rise to negative effects on economic development and welfare.

With reference to our findings, we close the chapter with a brief discussion of certain political factors which may provide in some instances a more plausible explanation of the suppression of basic trade union rights than those based on economic reasoning. We conclude that a social clause on basic trade union rights can be seen as an act of solidarity with foreign workers that do not have such rights. However its protective effects are considered to be rather dubious.

2.2. Basic Trade Union Rights in Newly Industrialised Countries – Some Indications of the Present State

In this section, we will look at the present situation concerning basic trade union rights in some NICs in Latin America and Southeast Asia.[13] In many countries in these parts of the world, trade union activities are not accepted by the ruling parties. Trade union members and their leaders are often arrested on no other grounds than their union activities, even though officially other reasons may be given by the authorities. The scanty and unreliable information that is available on this subject need not detain us any further. Instead we will restrict ourselves to the legal aspects of basic trade union rights.[14] However, in this case as well, unbiased information is rare due to the existence of strong political interests. Therefore, it is important to stress that the aim of this section is primarily to give some indication of the legal situation regarding basic trade union rights, as defined by ILO conventions nos. 87 and 98, in some less developed countries that have made great progress in industrial production and exportation during the last decades.

Among the non-European NICs, Mexico has ratified ILO convention no. 87, Brazil and Singapore convention no. 98 and Hong Kong has applied convention no. 98 without restrictions in its non-metropolitan territories, while convention no. 87 has been only partially applied in Hong Kong.[15] It should also be noted that in countries that have not ratified the conventions on basic trade union rights, great possibilities for various types of trade union activities may exist. In fact, some sort of trade union movement does exist in all NICs. However, as a rule, many restrictions have been imposed on the formation and operation of trade unions.

Although a country has ratified the conventions on basic trade union rights, this does not automatically mean that workers have the right freely to decide on their union formation and activities. For instance, in Brazil, trade unions and their activities are more or less completely controlled by the government. According to Cesarino and Cardone 'trade unions are almost a division of Government'.[16]

The governmental influence over trade union rights often starts by demanding registration or prior authorisation before an association of workers may act as a trade union. This is of course an efficient way of curtailing the possibilities of trade unionism. Hence, it is also in conflict with the contents of ILO convention no. 87. However, a legal demand for registration or authorisation might be nothing more than a formality. This seems to be the case for instance in Hong Kong, whereas in Brazil, Mexico and Singapore it is obviously more than that. In these countries, the application for registration can be refused. In Brazil, there may only be one union for workers in a specific area, i.e. for 'individuals belonging to the same category or exercising the same profession' in the specific territory where the union demands permission to work.[17] Trade union recognition will therefore be given to the most representative association of workers. As regards Singapore, the registration of a trade union may be cancelled by the Registrar if there are many unions in a specific trade, occupation or industry and he is of the opinion that the number of unions is too large with respect to what is optimal for the workers. In such cases, the Registrar has the ability to cancel the registration of all unions but one.[18]

Another restriction concerning the registration of trade unions is that the law in many countries includes minimum membership requirements for an association of workers to be recognised as a trade union. For instance, in Mexico, registration may be denied if there are less than 20 members of the association.[19] In Singapore, the union requirement states that at least 50 per cent of the workers concerned should be members of the union,[20] whereas, as a rule, more than one-third of the workers in a specific area have to be members if an association is to be recognised as a trade union in Brazil.[21] Obviously, minimum membership requirements effectively restrict the number of unions. On the one hand, this may provide greater strength for the unions that obtain registration than would have been the case with a high degree of union pluralism. On the other hand, pluralism means competition and competition gives rise to efficiency and can also be seen as a sort of guarantee against employer controlled union monopoly.

In connection with the legal restraints on the formation of trade unions, we should also notice that there may be rules governing the types of unions that may exist and the categories of workers that may affiliate. For instance, in Brazil, civil servants may not form unions,[22] whereas the laws of Mexico state that unions of public servants should cover workers employed in the same governmental unit.[23]

Up to now we have only dealt with the right of workers to form trade unions. The same type of restrictions as have been described above can be found in the laws on federations and confederations. For instance, in Hong Kong and Brazil, there are minimum requirements for registering a federation.[24] In Hong Kong, the unions in a federation must consist of workers from the same trade or industry.[25] Furthermore, in Brazil, the federations are restricted to cover unions in a specific state of the country while federations of trade unions from different trades or industries may not join together in a confederation,[26] whereas in Mexico unions of workers in the public sector may not affiliate with unions of workers employed in private enterprises.[27]

Great differences can also be found, among the countries concerned, in relation to the workers' right to collective bargaining. For instance, in Mexico, the law prescribes the employers to negotiate and make collective agreements with the unions,[28] whereas there is no such obligation in Brazil.[29] Furthermore, it is evident that in some countries the subjects of collective bargaining are severely restricted. For instance, in Singapore, one may not bargain collectively on questions of workers' promotion and dismissal, nor may the organisations in the labour market make agreements on clauses concerning terms and working conditions that are superior to those that can be found in the national legislation, without the permission of the competent minister,[30] whereas in Brazil there are severe restrictions placed on establishing collective agreements on wages. Here wages may not be changed more than once a year. Furthermore, they are not allowed to be raised by more than the increase in the cost of living, an adjustment which is carefully defined.[31]

The list of restrictions concerning the workers' rights to form and act through trade unions in the NICs outside Europe can be extended. We should not forget that in all these countries there are so-called 'Export Processing Zones' in which special laws apply.[32] As a rule, the laws on basic trade union rights are more restrictive in these zones than is the case in the rest of the country. However, the rather incomplete examples above give a clear insight into the problems that confront workers in their struggle for basic trade union rights in the NICs concerned.

Summary

From an empirical point of view, there is clearly a basis for the incorporation of a social clause on basic trade union rights in the rules that govern international trade. If such a clause was introduced, some of the developing countries, that have made great progress as producers and exporters of manufactures in the last decades, would face a choice between paving the way for trade unions by changing their labour market legislation or running the risk of facing trade barriers in their export markets due to the non-existence or severe curtailment of basic trade union rights.

2.3 Basic Trade Union Rights – Necessary but not Sufficient Conditions for Trade Union Activities

Trade union membership is often very low in developing countries where the legal restrictions on basic trade union rights are relatively limited. The weakness of trade unions in developing countries is sometimes explained by reference to the smallness of the industrial working class. However, in the case of industrialised developing countries, this explanation is only of minor significance. The explanation for low trade union membership and weak union activity must be found elsewhere.

According to Caire, the workers in many developing countries do not have 'a real sense of commitment'.[33] This implies that they stay at a specific job for only a short period, then leave for other activities. This of course gives rise to great problems for the trade unions both in terms of their recruitment of members and also in motivating their members for different trade union activities.

Illiteracy is also important in explaining why workers do not try to improve their working conditions through union activities. It makes workers passive at their work place and, according to

Caire, is 'the greatest obstacle to unionism'.[34] Of course illiteracy also implies problems for the recruitment of trade union leaders. In Asia, this problem has been 'solved' by taking the leaders from outside the unions' normal field of recruitment.[35] For instance, many union leaders are former politicians, lawyers and teachers. This type of recruitment does not have entirely positive implications for the unions, since there is an obvious risk that the leaders and the members have different aims for their unions. If this is the case, the potential members may be discouraged and the union may be weakened.

The weakness of trade unions in developing countries is also a consequence of the fact that as a rule existing trade union activities are concentrated at the particular plant or undertaking where the members work. This makes the unions small and weak. For instance, this is the case in Hong Kong where in 1973 some 70,000 workers out of a total manufacturing labour force of 750,000 workers were members of one of the 90 trade unions that existed in this part of the economy.[36] Furthermore, unions' collaboration in federations and confederations is relatively uncommon in many developing countries. This may well be a direct consequence of the labour market legislation in the countries in question.

In many less developed countries there is often a strong politicisation of the trade unions. Once again an example can be drawn from the situation in Hong Kong where the trade unions can be classified into three groups: the unions that are members of Hong Kong Federation of Trade Unions, which is a Communist organisation, the unions that are members of Hong Kong and Kowloon Trade Union Council, which is an organisation on the right of the political scene and finally the politically neutral trade unions of Hong Kong.[37] This strong politicisation easily gives rise to rivalries between different unions, thereby reducing other and more basic union activities which in turn tend to reduce the attractiveness of the existing trade unions.

In addition to the problems connected with union activities in many developing countries, we should also take into account their lack of financial resources. On the one hand, this is a consequence of the low number of members that often characterises the trade unions in these countries. On the other hand, this lack of financial resources weakens trade union activities. As a result, the attractiveness of the unions is further reduced so that the number of members is kept low, which in turn implies that the financial base is also kept at a low level. Consequently, the unions easily may find themselves in a situation where the possibilities for growth disappear as a result of the lack of financial resources.

Summary

Although basic trade union rights are necessary for the existence of trade unions, they are not sufficient for the development of trade unions and trade union activities. Illiteracy, politicisation of unions and lack of financial resources are some important factors that hamper the development of unions in less developed countries.

2.4 Trade Unions and Economic Development

As already noted, at the beginning of the industrialisation process, the opposition against the right of the workers to organise was supported by economists. More recently, critical views have also been advanced concerning basic trade union rights in less developed countries.[38] These views are based mainly on the conflict between wages and profits. Since economic growth and thereby also economic development depends on the rate of investment, and as this depends on the level of savings in the economy, income distribution can be critical for the growth aspect of economic development.[39] If one accepts this view and assumes that wage earners have a higher propensity to consume than capital owners, there is immediately a conflict between the efforts of trade unions to raise wages and the rate of investment. Thereby, a conflict also arises between unions and economic growth.

In addition to this negative influence of trade unions, such unions can also be claimed to have a negative impact on worker productivity.[40] First, it is obvious that in the case of trade unionism, some workers and managers have to work on bargaining and related questions instead of taking part in the pure production activities. Average productivity thereby decreases when a union is introduced, *ceteris paribus*. Secondly, trade unions are said to impose make-work rules. This often means that there are imposed 'limits on the load handled by workers, restrictions of the tasks performed by employees in given occupations, requirements that work be done twice or that unnecessary work be done, requirements for unneeded standby crews or crews of excessive size, enforcement of loose production standards or limits on work pace, and interference with technological changes sought by management'.[41] Thirdly, it is sometimes argued that trade unions give rise to more open discontent and open conflicts such as strikes.

However, economic development is not just a question of growth. Meier defines economic development as 'the process whereby the real per capita income of a country increases over a long period of time – subject to the stipulations that the number below an "absolute poverty line" does not increase, and that the distribution of income does not become more unequal'.[42] But even if we restrict our treatment of economic development to economic growth the above line of argument only tells part of the story.

First, the question may arise whether trade unions in developing countries really can raise wages. In many developing countries the possibilities seem to be small. The reason is the frequent existence of what Lewis has called an 'unlimited supply of labour'.[43] In such cases the unions have no opportunity to raise wages for unskilled workers above the wage rate that employers have to pay to make workers move out of the informal sector of the economy, unless the unions succeed in obtaining an efficient minimum wage legislation.

Secondly, in cases when wages really can be raised by trade union activities, the negative influence on investments and economic growth may be weakened by the improvements to the human capital of the workers concerned, which can arise as a consequence of the increased wages and the accompanying improved standard of living. There are also economists who argue that higher wages may influence economic growth positively by forcing producers to become more efficient in order to keep profits unchanged.[44] However, in order for this to be a valid argument in favour of trade unions one must explain why producers did not maximise profits when there were no unions and wages were lower. In my opinion, this argument seems to be too weak in its general version even though it can be of interest in cases when producers are not assumed to maximise profits but to satisfy other aims with their production activities.

Trade unions can also play an important role in providing and exchanging information in a production unit. Thereby a union can make the management aware of potential changes that could improve the situation of the workers at the same time as it could improve the efficiency of production. Furthermore, this may reduce labour turnover in the production unit concerned. Thereby, specific company training schemes and other forms of investments in human capital become more profitable than is the case when worker discontent results in 'quits'. Quits are a costly way to provide information on working conditions both from the point of view of the employee and the employer concerned but it is the major alternative to the above form of worker-management information by means of trade unions.[45] Closely related to this argument is that trade unions tend to give rise to more open discontent and strikes. However, to evaluate this argument it is important to keep in mind that absence of open discontent, conflicts and strikes does not mean that discontent does not exist, nor that no workdays are lost due to such discontent. In this case it is important to look closer at the changes in the frequency of absenteeism, leaving the job without notice, quits, laziness on the job, sabotage, etc.[46]

Furthermore, by collective bargaining and by monitoring the bargained contracts, the unions may also be able to change the attitude of the workers and improve job motivation. These effects of trade unions, that mainly arise from the unions' role as a link in the information process between workers and management, tend to increase the productivity of workers and the efficiency of the production units. Consequently, from this point of view, trade union activity also tends to contribute to the rate of economic growth.

As mentioned above, economic development is not just a question of economic growth. Changes of income distribution and of social conditions are also important parts of economic development. However, the weighting of these aspects in relation to growth is a question of the preferences of the economy concerned. If we assume that these preferences can be represented by a social welfare function and that the politicians try to maximise the social welfare of the economy, the welfare function of the economy must be known. In the real world we cannot expect to find a unique answer to the question of the form of this function. As a consequence, the politicians have to adopt some function which they think reflects the welfare of the economy. It is not too strong an assumption to make that politicians tend to use a social welfare function in which their own preferences are given a high priority. In non-democratic countries, these tendencies can be expected to be predominant. This may seem to imply an obvious risk that workers and individuals at lower positions in the society are given little attention and that workers' efforts to form and act through trade unions are suppressed. In a fairly recent study, Caire concludes that trade unions must be looked upon as an important means for the workers to vindicate their interests in the process of economic development.[47] In this connection reference can also be made to an ILO report on freedom of association:

> If it is accepted that economic development has social objectives, trade unions will always have a proper role to play in it. There is no substitute for trade unions as the workers' own instrument for obtaining a more equitable share of the fruits of economic progress.[48]

The justification of trade unions in a democratic or just society can also be analysed from a philosophical point of view. In his book, *A Theory of Justice*, Rawls derives principles of justice that ought to govern coexistence in a just society. By assuming that the individuals of the society are in a position where they do not know which place each one of them will have in the society for which they are going to determine the ruling principles, Rawls derives that agreement can be reached on the principle that in a fair society 'each person is to have an equal right to the most extensive total system of equal basic liberties compatible with a similar system of liberty for all'.[49]

In reality, a set of basic liberties that satisfies this fundamental principle of justice is contained in the UN declarations and conventions on human rights. It is worth noting that even before the UN declarations and conventions existed, the ILO had adopted human rights conventions for the labour market, among which we find conventions on basic trade union rights.[50] Consequently, in a just society governed by the fundamental principle of liberty referred to above, there seems to be a central place for basic trade union rights. In a society where basic trade union rights are absent or restricted, it can be concluded that individual freedom is also restricted. Therefore, a social clause on these rights can be seen as an external pressure for liberty.

Summary

The controversy regarding the relationship between basic trade union rights and economic development rests upon a presumed conflict between trade unions and the growth aspect of economic development. From the above analysis, we conclude that the existence of such a conflict is doubtful. The effects on economic growth should not be analysed solely from a narrow perspective including the trade union influence on wages. The analysis has to be extended so that it also takes into account the effects on worker-management relations, workers' morale and motivation, etc. If this is done, the negative relationship that is often presumed to exist between trade unionism and economic growth is weakened and we cannot exclude the possibility that the relationship turns out to be positive.

Furthermore, in a democratic society where due attention is paid to human rights, basic trade union rights can be claimed to have a central place. From this point of view, a social clause on such rights can be classified as a means of solidarity with foreign workers now living in countries where there are restrictions placed on the workers' rights to form and act through unions.

2.5 Trade Unions and Economic Welfare

In the economic literature there has long existed a view that a trade union gives rise to social losses in the same way as a monopoly firm in the commodity market.[51] An example of this view has been presented by Levis Kochin who concludes that:

> Unions have obtained higher wages for their members. The cost to society of these higher wages are caused by (1) A misallocation of labor – too little employment at unionized work and too much elsewhere (2) Rent Dissipation – the cost of competition for union jobs and of efforts to create and destroy unions (3) Rigidity – union rules cause an increase in the rigidity of work practice and of wages.[52]

In this section we will take a closer look at the theoretical analysis that lies behind these results.

Is Perfect Competition the Alternative?

The analysis of the social losses caused by trade unions starts from the implicit assumption that in the absence of trade unions the labour market can be characterised as being perfectly competitive. It is then relatively easy to demonstrate that there is a risk of losses of the first type mentioned by Kochin. To illustrate this we use Figure 2.1.

If the market is characterised by perfect competition, equilibrium in Figure 2.1 is attained at the point of intersection of the demand and supply curves denoted L^D and L^S respectively, and L_c units of labour will be employed at the competitive wage w_c. There will then be a social surplus equal to the area GBH.

Figure 2.1

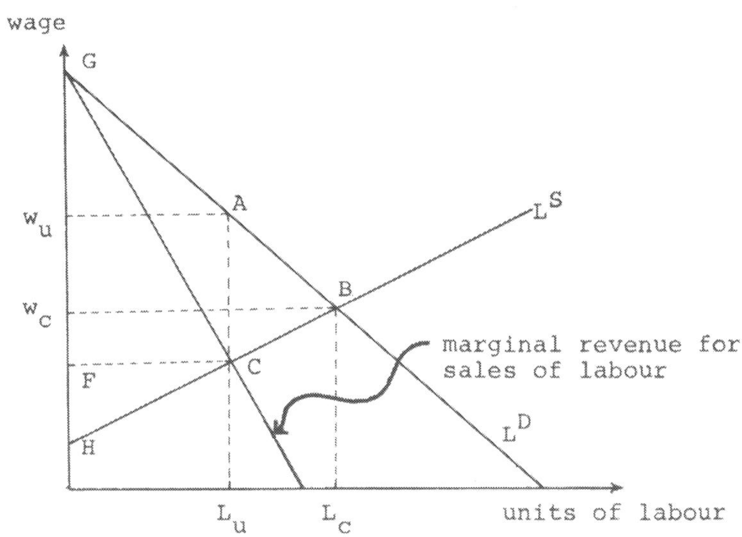

If a trade union is formed and obtains control over the supply of labour the market equilibrium will change. As the sole seller of labour, the union knows that in order to maximise the surplus, defined as the difference between the sum of wages and the opportunity cost of labour (represented by the curve L^S), the employment level should be determined by the intersection of the curves describing the marginal revenue for sales of labour and the supply of labour. Consequently, with a surplus maximising union, L_u units of labour will be employed at the wage w_u. Comparing this situation with that of perfect competition, we find that there are employers demanding labour who are willing to pay a wage in excess of the opportunity cost of labour. From a welfare point of view, we note that the surplus to the employers will be reduced from GBw_c to GAw_u, whereas the surplus to the workers will increase from HBw_c to $HCAw_u$. Thus, the emergence of the union will give rise to a social loss equal to the area ABC in Figure 2.1.

It is important to remember that the above analysis begins from the assumption that perfect competition prevails in the labour market. However, as a rule, the assumption of perfect competition is not valid in labour markets.[53] In many countries without trade unions we would expect to find a monopsony in the labour market, especially if we restrict the perspective to local and regional markets. If a trade union is formed in a labour market characterised by a monopsony the effects will differ radically from those derived and illustrated in Figure 2.1. The employer knows that he has to bid up the wage if he wants to use more labour. If perfect wage discrimination cannot be applied, the employer also knows that it is not only the last worker but also all workers previously employed who will receive the higher wage. In Figure 2.2 the incremental labour cost associated with increased employment is described by the marginal cost curve for labour. The monopsonist maximises profits at the employment level where

Figure 2.2

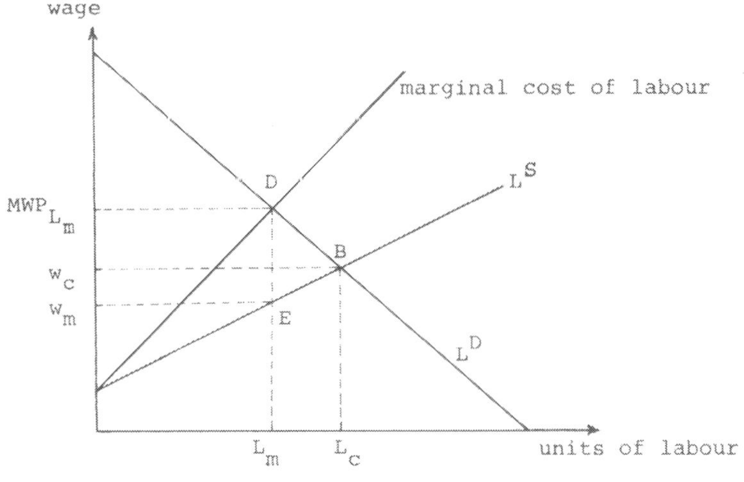

the curves describing the marginal cost of labour and the demand for labour intersect. In Figure 2.2, this gives employment of L_m units of labour at the wage w_m. There is a social loss in this market situation represented by the area DBE.

An interesting question is what happens to this loss when the workers form a trade union for collective action in the labour market. It is obvious that there will be a change in the social loss. However, whether this change is positive or negative depends on the outcome of the bargaining process in the new situation. In the case where the agreed wage is less than what the monopsonist was willing to pay for the employment of L_m units of labour, MWP_{L_m}, the social loss will be reduced since employment will increase towards the competitive level, L_c. In fact, it may be the case that a situation identical to the competitive equilibrium arises and the social loss is eliminated by trade union activities. From this we can see that if there is initially a monopsony in the labour market, the formation of trade unions cannot be generally rejected by reference to the traditional analysis of loss under monopoly. In fact, the formation of a trade union may well give rise to increased employment and production, and thereby also give rise to a social gain.[54]

Do Trade Unions Give Rise to Socially Valuable By-products?

We now turn to the second cause of social losses due to trade unions referred to by Kochin. To the loss ABC in Figure 2.1 Kochin, with reference to Tullock and Posner,[55] adds a social loss described by the area w_uACF.[56] This loss is made up of 'the expenses incurred in efforts to form, maintain and obtain entry into unions as well as the costs incurred in efforts to obstruct, destroy, harass or otherwise hinder the efforts of trade unions to maintain wages above those that would exist in the absence of union monopoly'.[57] One may raise objections to this analysis. First, this loss may also exist in the absence of trade unions if workers try to establish a union but fail to do so because of, for instance, the employers' efforts to prevent unionisation. Therefore, even though a labour market is characterised by perfect competition, resources may be used for the same type of activities underlying the loss w_uACF in Figure 2.1. Furthermore, on the basis of Posner's analysis of the assumptions necessary for the existence of a loss of size w_uACF in a monopoly market, it emerges that one of the critical assumptions is that 'the costs incurred in obtaining a monopoly have no socially valuable by-products'.[58] It is then important to investigate whether the formation of a trade union gives rise to such by-products, and thereby reduces, or even eliminates, this type of loss.

In the previous section on basic trade union rights and economic development, we have already described different types of by-products of trade unions. Examples are the unions' effects on worker-management relations, on company training schemes and on workers' morale and motivation. On the other hand, trade unions may also give rise to negative by-products. The resources devoted to bargaining and related questions, and the imposition of make-work rules are examples of such effects.

Consequently, as was the case with the relationship between trade unions and economic development, the relationship between trade unions and economic efficiency and welfare cannot be analysed from a narrow perspective including only the union influence on wages. The analysis must also take into account the socially valuable by-products of unions. If this is done, the necessary assumption behind the existence of the social loss w_uACF, namely that the monopoly, i.e. the trade union, does not give rise to socially valuable by-products is not satisfied.

Working Conditions as Local Public Goods.

Finally, we will take up one aspect that as a rule is totally neglected in analyses of the welfare effects of trade unions. Many specific working conditions apply to all workers in a given production unit and exclusion is often impossible or very expensive. This is the case, for example, with different aspects of occupational health and safety. In such cases working conditions can be characterised as local public goods. From economic theory, it is well known that private optimisation easily gives rise to an inoptimal production of public goods.[59] In cases where the explicit valuations of individual consumers, as reflected by, say, interviews, are connected with a payment responsibility, the revealed demand will be less than the true demand. Consequently production of the public good will be below the optimal level.

In the same way, we can expect that working conditions with public good characteristics are inoptimal in a monopsonistic labour market.[60] When workers do not express their preferences over various working conditions collectively, non-pecuniary working conditions characterised by non-excludability cannot be differentiated among the workers at the same workplace. Therefore, the quality of such working conditions, that arise out of the monopsonist's profit maximisation, will be based on the marginal worker's marginal valuation of these working conditions and not on all workers' valuations which would be the relevant ones from a social welfare, or social surplus, point of view. There is empirical evidence which indicates that intramarginal workers are older and wealthier than marginal workers and therefore tend to place a greater valuation on non-pecuniary working conditions.[61] When this is the case, non-pecuniary working conditions characterised by non-excludability will be substandard in monopsonistic labour markets.

If workers in a specific workplace form a union and act collectively in negotiations with their employer, a situation of bilateral monopoly arises. The outcome of the resulting bargaining process, with respect to various working conditions, depends on the relative strength of the two parties involved and is in principle indeterminate. As demonstrated in the preceding section, the formation of a trade union in a monopsonistic labour market may, but need not, give rise to increased social surplus and welfare. In fact, we found that it is possible that it will give rise to a socially optimal outcome. In the case when non-pecuniary working conditions characterised by non-excludability are present there is an increased likelihood that a positive welfare effect will arise out of the formation of a trade union in a monopsonistic labour market. The reason is that the trade union attitude towards various working conditions will be based on all workers' valuations rather than on the valuation of the marginal worker.

Summary

Trade unions are often claimed to give rise to social losses. A closer look at the analyses behind these findings gives rise to many objections and the social losses become very doubtful.

First, if the labour market in question can be characterised in the absence of trade unions as a monopsonistic market, it is very doubtful if there will be a social loss due to increased misallocation of labour when trade unions are formed. In fact, in such a labour market situation the formation of trade unions may well result in a reduced misallocation of labour and, thereby, give rise to social net gains.

Secondly, the 'rent dissipation' cause of social losses is also of doubtful significance. According to Posner, this loss can only arise if the formation of the monopoly, here the trade union, has no socially valuable by-products. The formation of a trade union certainly has such by-products.

Thirdly, since important working conditions have the character of local public goods, collective action is often needed when working conditions are being determined in order to avoid a misallocation of resources. For such action, some form of trade union is needed. As a rule, this aspect of unions is not dealt with at all in analyses of the social losses due to trade unions.

Finally, it should be noted that when there is an unlimited supply of labour in the economy at the relevant wage levels, there is no chance for a trade union to obtain monopoly power. Consequently, trade union activities in the labour market cannot give rise to a social loss due to an increased misallocation of labour unless the unions are able to obtain wage improvements or cost-increasing changes in other working conditions by legislative measures.

2.6 Concluding Remarks

By looking at the juridical situation of basic trade union rights in some newly industrialised countries, we have noted that workers' rights to form and act through trade unions are often severely restricted by law. One of the main economic arguments against unions is based on a presumed conflict between trade unionism and economic development. Our study of the different analyses, presented by economists, of the effects of unionism on factors that are of importance for economic growth, leads to the conclusion that there is no clear-cut negative relationship between trade union activities and economic development.

Other arguments against trade unions are based on welfare economic considerations. These arguments have been found to be too weak to form a general basis for restrictions on basic trade union rights. Furthermore, basic trade union rights can be claimed to be natural ingredients in democratic societies where individual freedom and human rights are respected.

Our conclusion that, as a rule, there is no clear-cut negative relationship between trade unionism and economic development, nor any welfare economic arguments against such unions strong enough to motivate restrictions of basic trade union rights, raises the question whether there are really any rational arguments for the regimes, for instance in newly industrialised countries, to impose legal restraints on these rights. The answer may well be found in the field of politics. If workers are guaranteed basic trade union rights, the regimes may believe that they can expect a growing organised opposition arising out of the unions. This would inevitably reduce the regime's freedom of operation. It does not seem too strong an assumption to make that, as a rule, political aspects of trade unionism provide a better explanation of the existing restrictions on basic trade union rights than the economic aspects on which we have been concentrating in this chapter.

From this point of view, a social clause on basic trade union rights can be classified as an act of solidarity with foreign workers in countries where such rights do not exist. However, as a protective means, such a clause is doubtful. First, it should be noted that the existence of basic trade union rights is far from sufficient for trade union activities to arise. Secondly, the existence of union activities does not necessarily give rise to increased costs of production and reduced competitive strength in the international market. This is particularly the case if the export economies concerned have a labour market characterised by an unlimited supply of labour. Finally, in the case when trade unions exert a real influence on wages and other labour-related costs of production, it is possible that this is done via a process of collective bargaining under market conditions that can be characterised as a bilateral monopoly. If so, we cannot exclude the possibility that production for export may increase.

Notes

1. For instance, see Braun (1950), pp. 17f.
2. For instance, see Webb (1902), Part III, Ch. 1 and Robbins (1978), pp. 5f.
3. Braun (1950), pp. 24f.
4. Ibid.
5. For the complete text, see for instance ILO (1975).
6. Convention no. 87, article 2.
7. Convention no. 87, article 3.
8. Convention no. 87, article 3.
9. Convention no. 87, article 5.
10. Convention no. 98, article 1.
11. Convention no. 98, article 4.

12. Information received from ILO.

13. The countries dealt with in this section are Brazil, Mexico, Hong Kong and Singapore.

14. Erstling (1977), ILO (1975), Blanpain (1979).

15. Information received from ILO and country surveys in Blanpain (1979). According to Lethbridge and Hong, federations may not be formed in the non-metropolitan territory of Hong Kong.

16. Cesarino and Cardone (1979), p. 132.

17. Ibid., p. 137.

18. Erstling (1977), p. 27.

19. Castillo (1979), p. 101.

20. Axelsson and Perjus (1978), p. 149. According to Erstling more than seven members are required to form a union (Erstling (1977), p. 3).

21. Cesarino and Cardone (1979), p. 137.

22. Ibid., p. 131.

23. Erstling (1977), p. 8.

24. Lethbridge and Hong (1979), p. 171, Cesarino and Cardone (1979), p. 139 and Erstling (1977), p. 30.

25. Lethbridge and Hong (1979), p. 30.

26. Cesarino and Cardone (1979), pp. 139, 140.

27. Erstling (1977), p. 33.

28. Castillo (1979), p. 109.

29. Cesarino and Cardone (1979), p. 142.

30. ILO (1975), pp. 36, 37.

31. Cesarino and Cardone (1979), p. 142.

32. For instance, see Fröbel *et al.* (1977), Landsorganisationen (1980).

33. Caire (1977), pp. 75f.

34. Ibid., p. 76.

35. Ibid., p. 76.

36. Axelsson and Perjus (1978), p. 65.

37. Ibid.

38. See e.g. deSchweinitz (1959). See also Caire (1977), pp. 47f and Mehta (1957).

39. For a survey of economic theories on growth and capital accumulation, see Lundahl (1979).

40. See e.g. Dunlop (1958), Rees (1962), Slichter *et al.* (1960) for analyses of the relationship between the existence of trade unions and worker productivity. See also Brown and Medoff (1978) and Clark (1980) for recent estimates of the union impact on worker productivity in the US manufacturing industry and the US cement industry, respectively.

41. Brown and Medoff (1978), p. 359.

42. Meier (1976), p. 6.

43. Lewis (1954).

44. Sturmthal (1960).

45. Freeman (1976).

46. According to Kassalow (1969), p. 159: 'The more firmly the labour movement is institutionalized and "accepted", particularly in the sphere of labour-management relations, the greater the likelihood that there will be fewer strikes.' See also Parker (1920), p. 76: 'Resistance by the worker to an employer's labour policy takes one of two forms: either an open and formal revolt, such as a strike; or an instinctive and often unconscious exercise of the "strike in detail" – simply drifting off the job.'

47. Caire (1977), pp. 60f. See also Galenson (1959), p. 18.

48. ILO (1971), p. 34.

49. Rawls (1973), p. 60.

50. For a description of the international work on human rights, see e.g. Haas (1970), Jenks (1960) and Luard (1967).

51. Kochin (1980), p. 325. The same line of argument can be found for instance in Burton (1978). See also Reynolds (1981) and references therein. The analysis in this section relies heavily on Hansson (1982).

52. Kochin (1980), p. 325.

53. For instance, see Mortensen (1970) and Viscusi (1979, 1980).

54. In the same way, the formation of an employer organisation may give rise to social gains in a labour market with a trade union monopoly.

55. Tullock (1967), Posner (1975).

56. Kochin (1980), p. 325.

57. Ibid.

58. Posner (1975), p. 809.

59. For instance, see Samuelson (1954).

60. See Viscusi (1980); see also Drèze (1976).

61. See Viscusi (1980) and references therein.

3 SOCIAL CLAUSES ON SPECIFIC WORKING CONDITIONS

3.1 Introduction

Although basic trade union rights are given great emphasis in the demands for an incorporation of labour standards in the rules that govern international trade, it is generally considered that labour standards on specific working conditions have a greater chance of being accepted for incorporation.[1] Without making any judgements on the likelihood of getting various types of labour standards accepted as part of the rules governing international trade, we will in this chapter take a closer look at the economic effects of introducing labour standards or social clauses on specific working conditions in trade policy. The conditions to be analysed are wages, hours of work, child labour and occupational health and safety.[2] In conjunction with the analysis a few brief details will be provided on the present state of the working conditions in question in some newly industrialised countries as well as in some 'old' industrialised countries, in order to demonstrate the large differences in working conditions that exist among countries, differences that also make up the empirical basis for the demands for social clauses. However, before we proceed with the analysis of social clauses on specific working conditions, we will present the analytical framework of this chapter.

3.2 The Analytical Framework

The aims of the present study were described in Chapter 1. These were *inter alia* to analyse the effects on employment, national income and income distribution in economies that have had to change their working conditions following the incorporation of social clauses in trade policy. We will also compare these effects with the effects of traditional trade policy measures. To analyse these types of economic effects a general equilibrium approach seems warranted. In international economics, general equilibrium analyses are traditionally worked out within different varieties of a 'two-by-two-by-two model'. This type of model describes an economy consisting of two sectors of production, each one producing one homogeneous commodity with two factors of production. The 'two-ness' of the model is often extended to include a two-country world.

The two-by-two-by-two model has been criticised from different points of view. One of the critics, Frank Graham, states that: 'one of the very strongest reasons for rejection of the classical doctrines is that the classicists themselves made their analysis in such simple terms (two-country, two-commodity trade) and then erroneously projected their results into complex trading situations.'[3] Thus, while often it may be appropriate to take this type of model as a point of departure, it has certainly to be extended to analyse a number of important problems in international economics.[4] For example, the two-country assumption makes it impossible to analyse the problems of customs unions. The assumption of only two commodities rules out the possibility of analysing the problem of the optimal tariff structures. Furthermore, this assumption implies problems for the incorporation of non-traded goods in the analysis of international trade. In a two-commodity model of international trade both commodities have to be traded goods since imports have to be paid for by exports. The assumption of two commodities also rules out the possibility of complementarity between products in both production and consumption, i.e. the commodities have to be substitutes. In a multi-commodity world this need not be the case.

The two-by-two-by-two model also seems to be too restrictive for the purposes of the present study. The demands for social clauses have emphasised working conditions in the industrial export sector. Consequently, it would seem appropriate to work with models that contain at least two industrial sectors, of which one would be covered by the social clauses. However, an agricultural sector will also be included in our model, since NICs and other less developed countries can be expected to dominate the group of countries that will be confronted with the different social clauses. As a rule, agriculture is the major sector in these countries.

A three-sector model that can be taken as a starting point for our formal analysis has been presented by Gruen and Corden in their article, 'A Tariff that Worsens the Terms of Trade'.[5] Their model describes an economy with two agricultural and one manufacturing sector. The agricultural sectors use labour and land whereas labour and capital are used in manufacturing. In this chapter we will work with an elaborated version of Gruen's and Corden's model.

First, as mentioned above, we assume that the analysed economy consists of one agricultural and two industrial sectors. Furthermore, our analysis will deal with economies with different labour market characteristics. In one type of economy, the *full employment economy*, there is a given labour force that is constantly fully employed. In this type of economy, the wage rate is always adjusted so that full employment is established. This is the traditional way of dealing with the labour market in general equilibrium models. However, as developing countries can be expected to be the countries most affected by an incorporation of social clauses in trade policy, and as many of these countries have high levels of unemployment, an analysis based on a model where full employment is assumed may often be inappropriate. Consequently, our analysis will also be carried out using models that allow permanent unemployment. We call this type of economy a *labour surplus economy*.[6] In such an economy, we assume the wage rate to be exogenously determined. For instance, this wage rate can be determined by a minimum wage law or by the consumption standard that a worker can obtain in activities outside the economy's three formal sectors of production. Assuming that there is a labour surplus at the current real wage, there will be a reservoir of workers who have failed to get employment in the three formal sectors at that wage level.[7] So in fact, we can say that besides the formal sectors of production, there is a fourth, informal, sector in the economy.

A general equilibrium model describing this type of labour market situation for a two-sector economy has been presented by Batra and Seth in their article, 'Unemployment, Tariffs and the Theory of International Trade'.[8] By working with production functions that display decreasing returns to scale, Batra and Seth can derive a uniquely determined production without complete specialisation.

In the following analysis, we will combine the approach of Batra and Seth, which allows for permanent unemployment without necessarily leading to complete specialisation or production indeterminacy, with the basic production structure of the model by Gruen and Corden. Our analysis will be worked out by means of models that describe a three-sector economy containing one agricultural sector, A, and two industrial sectors, manufacturing, M and extractive industry, E. The agricultural sector is assumed to use labour, L, and land, R, whereas in manufacturing and the extractive industry labour is assumed to be combined with capital, K. The different factors of production are all assumed to be homogeneous. The production functions for the three sectors of the economy can be written:

$$M = M(L_M, K_M, t_M)$$

$$E = E(L_E, K_E)$$

$$A = A(L_A, R_A)$$

where

L_i = use of labour in sector i, i = M, E, A

K_i = use of capital in sector i, i = M, E

R_A = use of land in agriculture

t_M = a parameter that represents the technology used in manufacturing

The production functions are assumed to be twice continuously differentiable in terms of their factors of production and in the case of the manufacturing industry in relation to its technology parameter as well.

The marginal productivities of the factors of production are assumed to be positive and decreasing. Furthermore, we assume that the marginal productivity of one factor of production increases when the use of other factors increase in the sector. Hence, it is assumed that:

$$M_L, M_K, E_L, E_K, A_L, \text{ and } A_R > 0$$

$$M_{KL}, E_{KL}, A_{RL} > 0$$

$$M_{LL}, M_{KK}, E_{LL}, E_{KK}, A_{LL}, \text{ and } A_{RR} < 0$$

Furthermore, the manufacturing industry and agriculture are both assumed to display constant returns to scale in the specified factors of production. For the extractive industry, however, we assume decreasing returns to scale in labour and capital, since it is expected that the most productive mines are utilised first. By this assumption we avoid the problem of complete specialisation and production indeterminacy in the industrial parts of labour surplus economies.

We also assume that all markets concerned, commodity markets as well as factor markets, with the exception of the labour market in labour surplus economies, are perfectly competitive.[9] Furthermore, in this chapter the commodity prices are assumed to be determined in the international commodity markets where the analysed economy is too small to have any influence. By this assumption, we can concentrate on the supply side of the economy when we analyse the effects of an incorporation of social clauses on specific working conditions. In Chapter 4, where we compare social clauses with traditional trade barriers, we will comment upon the effects of social clauses when the small country assumption is not satisfied.

Using the price of agricultural output as numeraire and assuming profit maximising producers, we derive the following necessary conditions for long run equilibrium in the two types of economies that we are going to analyse.

$$w = \bar{w} \tag{1}$$

$$\alpha w = p_M M_L (L_M, K_M, t_M) \tag{2}$$

$$w = p_E E_L (L_E, K_E) \tag{3}$$

$$w = A_L (L_A, R_A) \tag{4}$$

$$r_M = p_M M_K (L_M, K_M, t_M) \tag{5}$$

$$r_E = p_E E_K (L_E, K_E) \tag{6}$$

$$r_M = r_E \tag{7}$$

$$v = A_R (L_A, R_A) \tag{8}$$

$$K = K_M + K_E \tag{9}$$

$$R = R_A \tag{10}$$

$$L = L_M + L_E + L_A \tag{11}$$

where (1)–(10) belong to labour surplus economy and (2)–(11) to full employment economy and where

w = real wage rate

r_i = marginal return to capital in industry i, i = M, E

v = land rent

p_i = price of commodity i in terms of commodity A, i = M, E

α = w_M/w, where w is the wage rate in non-manufacturing sectors. Initially, i.e. before the social clauses have been introduced, the economy is assumed to be in a long run equilibrium where $\alpha = 1$

L, K and R denote the total labour force and the total amounts of capital and land in the economy
$\bar{w}$ denotes the exogenously determined real wage rate in a labour surplus economy

Once social clauses on various specific working conditions are incorporated in trade policy, changes are assumed to take place in the analysed economy in order to satisfy the requirements stated in the clauses. Thereby the initial equilibrium will be disturbed. The changes that have to take place are represented by changes in the exogenous variables in the two types of economies. We will return to these changes in each of the following sections of this chapter in conjunction with the analysis of the economic effects of an incorporation of social clauses on various working conditions.

The social clauses are assumed to be directed against the manufacturing industry of the economy. This assumption can be motivated by the fact that the recent demands for protectionism have mainly concerned manufactures and especially relatively labour-intensive manufactures.

In the following analysis, the assumptions made in relation to relative factor intensities are sometimes decisive for obtaining determinate and clear-cut results, especially in full employment economies. In these cases, we will assume manufacturing to be less capital-intensive than the extractive industry. Furthermore, throughout the chapter, we assume that the analysed social clauses do not give rise to factor intensity reversals. Thereby we assume away the possibility that abnormal effects may arise in full employment economies.[10] It is worth noting that this assumption is superfluous for the analysis of labour surplus economies, where there is no risk of such effects.

By elaborating the systems of equations for equilibrium in the two types of economies described above and taking total derivatives, a traditional comparative static analysis of the long run effects of an incorporation of social clauses can be worked out. However, in this study we will not follow this approach. Instead of deriving the long run effects in one step, we will follow the example of Mayer who, in an article entitled 'Short-Run and Long-Run Equilibrium for a Small Open Economy',[11] divided the analysis into two parts. First, we will analyse the short run or impact effects of an incorporation of social clauses in trade policy. By definition, in the short run, the allocation of capital is fixed between the two capital-using sectors of the economy. However, the exogenous disturbances, brought about by the incorporation of social clauses, will create a discrepancy between the returns to capital in the two sectors. Hence, the short run effects will induce capital reallocation. This process of adjustment to a new long run equilibrium will continue as long as the return to capital differs between the two industrial sectors and there is no complete specialisation in the industrial parts of the economy.

Let us now derive the systems of equations that are later to be solved for different exogenous changes of working conditions.

The Full Employment Economy

Starting with the full employment economy, we can substitute equations (9)–(11) into equations (2)–(6) and (8) in the system presented above. Thereby we obtain the following system of equations that is also assumed to describe the initial long run equilibrium of the economy.[12]

$$\alpha w = p_M M_L (L_M, K_M, t_M)$$

$$w = p_E E_L (L_E, K - K_M)$$

$$w = A_L (L - L_M - L_E, R)$$

$$r_M = p_M M_K (L_M, K_M, t_M)$$

$$r_E = p_E E_K (L_E, K - K_M)$$

$$r_M = r_E$$

$$v = A_R(L - L_M - L_E, R)$$

By total differentiation, keeping the price of E and the total amounts of capital and land constant, we derive the following system of equations:

$$w d\alpha + \alpha dw = M_L dp_M + p_M M_{LL} dL_M + p_M M_{LK} dK_M + p_M M_{Lt} dt_M \qquad (12)$$

$$dw = p_E E_{LL} dL_E - p_E E_{LK} dK_M \qquad (13)$$

$$dw = A_{LL} dL - A_{LL} dL_M - A_{LL} dL_E \qquad (14)$$

$$dr_M = M_K dp_M + p_M M_{KL} dL_M + p_M M_{KK} dK_M + p_M M_{Kt} dt_M \qquad (15)$$

$$dr_E = p_E E_{KL} dL_E - p_E E_{KK} dK_M \qquad (16)$$

$$dr_M = dr_E \qquad (17)$$

$$dv = A_{RL} dL - A_{RL} dL_M - A_{RL} dL_E \qquad (18)$$

As already mentioned, the following analysis will be divided into a short run analysis and an analysis of the long run adjustment effects. Since in the short run, the allocation of capital is fixed, $dK_M = 0$. Furthermore, due to the fixed allocation of capital, the introduction of various social clauses will, as a rule, give rise to a short run difference between the marginal returns to capital in the two capital-using industries. Consequently, in a short run analysis, equation (17) should be deleted.

As the resulting system of equations contains six linearly independent equations and six endogenous variables, dL_M, dL_E, dw, dr_M, dr_E and dv, we know that if there exists a solution to the system, it must be unique. In the following sections we assume that a solution does exist and solve this system of equations with respect to changes in different exogenous variables that represent various types of changes in the manufacturing industry.

When in the short run, a social clause gives rise to a difference in the marginal returns to capital between the two industries, there will in the longer run be a reallocation of capital and the economy will adjust towards a new long run equilibrium. To analyse the effects of this adjustment on various endogenous variables, we solve the same system of equations as for the short run analysis but now with respect to exogenous changes in the manufacturing use of capital.[13]

The Labour Surplus Economy

In order to analyse a labour surplus economy, we substitute equations (1), (9) and (10) into equations (2)–(6) and (8). For this type of economy we set $\alpha = 1$ in equation (2) since wage differentials can be treated directly by working with different levels for the exogenous wages in each sector of the economy. By these elaborations we get the following system of equations, that is also assumed to describe the initial long run equilibrium of the economy:

$$\bar{w} = p_M M_L (L_M, K_M, t_M)$$

$$\bar{w} = p_E E_L (L_E, K - K_M)$$

$$\bar{w} = A_L (L_A, R)$$

$$r_M = p_M M_K (L_M, K_M, t_M)$$

$$r_E = p_E E_K (L_E, K - K_M)$$

$$r_M = r_E$$

$$v = A_R (L_A, R)$$

By total differentiation, keeping the price on E and the total amounts of capital and land constant, we get:

$$dw = M_L dp_M + p_M M_{LL} dL_M + p_M M_{LK} dK_M + p_M M_{Lt} dt_M \quad (19)$$

$$dw = p_E E_{LL} dL_E - p_E E_{LK} dK_M \quad (20)$$

$$dw = A_{LL} dL_A \quad (21)$$

$$dr_M = M_K dp_M + p_M M_{KL} dL_M + p_M M_{KK} dK_M + p_M M_{Kt} dt_M \quad (22)$$

$$dr_E = p_E E_{KL} dL_E - p_E E_{KK} dK_M \quad (23)$$

$$dr_M = dr_E \quad (24)$$

$$dv = A_{RL} dL_A \quad (25)$$

By the same line of reasoning as in the case of full employment economies we delete equation (24) in our analysis. We thereby obtain a system of equations for the labour surplus economy containing six linearly independent equations and six endogenous variables, dL_M, dL_E, dL_A, dr_M, dr_E and dv. Since the number of linearly independent equations equals the number of endogenous variables, we know that if a solution exists, it must be unique. Assuming that a solution exists, we can now solve the system of equations for the short run effects as well as for the long run adjustment effects that result from the introduction of social clauses on various specific working conditions.[14]

3.3 A Social Clause on Wages

In trade policy discussions concerning imports from developing countries, one argument that is frequently advanced by protectionists is that of cheap labour. According to this argument, export industries in many developing countries are said to be competitive in the international market due to an 'exploitation' of workers who are paid wages below their productivity and below a level that make a 'decent' living possible.[15] By incorporating a social clause on minimum wages in trade policy, a country's export opportunities will be restricted by traditional trade policy means, unless the level of wages in its export industry is raised, for instance by means of minimum wage legislation.

The question of minimum wage legislation has been discussed for many years. According to Blum, the first minimum wage legislation appeared in Australia in the nineteenth century.[16] During the twentieth century, this type of legislation has become more common. In fact, in 1980, 100 members of the International Labour Organisation had ratified the minimum wage conventions.[17] However, this does not mean that minimum wages do not exist in other countries, nor does it mean that the existence of minimum wages in these countries would leave them outside the scope of a social clause on wages.

One may wonder whether policy means like legislation on wages are needed at all. Why does the labour market not create wages that make a decent living possible for all workers? The main answer is probably associated with the existence of a large supply of low skilled workers in many of the countries where present wages are too low to obtain such a standard of living. In many developing countries there is a large excess supply of labour, even at low wage levels. Another answer can be the existence of monopsonies in the labour markets, which combined with a low mobility of labour makes it possible to keep wages low.

Considering the fact that many developing countries have a large labour surplus at the prevailing low levels of wages, one may wonder whether a social clause on wages will be sufficient to bring about changes that would improve the standard of living for the workers in these countries. This is a question that relates to the effects of an incorporation of a social clause on wages. However, before we proceed with the analysis of these effects, we will provide some indication of the level of wages in some non-European NICs.

The Present State

In this section we will present wage statistics relating to NICs outside Europe. We will concentrate on the situation in the manufacturing industry. Manufacturing wages will be analysed both with respect to their absolute levels and their development during the 1970s. In addition to a presentation of wage statistics for manufacturing as a whole, we shall also take a look at the statistics for those parts of the manufacturing industry where developing countries have been most successful in the international markets. Wage trends will also be compared with those of consumer prices in order to get some indication of changes in real wages.

From Table 3.1, we note that workers employed in the clothing industry are paid far below the average manufacturing wage in all NICs concerned. Furthermore, we note that in Brazil, workers employed in the specific industries mentioned in Table 3.1 have had a lower rate of wage increases than the average manufacturing worker between 1972 and 1976. Looking at wage trends in Mexico, we find quite the opposite situation. In all of the industries covered, apart from the leather industry, the workers have had wage increases above the average for manufacturing. Turning to the NICs in South-east Asia, we find that the pattern of development in Brazil is valid also for the wages paid to workers in South Korean manufacturing, except for workers employed in the transport equipment industry. In Singapore, workers in textiles as well as in the clothing and electronic industries have had more rapid wage increases in the 1970s than was the case for the

Table 3.1: Wages and Consumer Prices in Non-European NICs

	Brazil 1976		Mexico 1976		Hong Kong 1978		Singapore 1978		South Korea 1978		Taiwan 1978	
Nominal wages	(A)[1]	(B)[2,3]	(A)	(B)[4]	(A)	(B)	(A)	(B)[5]	(A)	(B)[5]	(A)	(B)[6]
Manufacturing	2,844	335	4,285	252	33.79	229	171	186	92,907	559	6,391	253
Textiles	1,654	274	4,254	275			145	230	74,480	559	5,631	247
Clothing	1,452	312	2,840	281			}120	207	60,878	504	5,215	265
Leather			3,925	250				185	68,600	495	5,380	284
Electronics	3,197	300					153	204	79,240	424	5,763	245
Transport equipment	3,833	274	4,534	279			242	179	154,636	766	8,442	268
Consumer prices												
General	254 1972 = 100		204 1970 = 100		185 1970 = 100		167 1971 = 100		261 1971 = 100		180 1973 = 100	
Food	267 1972 = 100		208 1970 = 100		195 1970 = 100		184 1971 = 100		300 1971 = 100		198 1973 = 100	

Notes:

1. (A) Absolute level. Monthly wage in all cases but Hong Kong where daily wage is given. Wages are given in the country's own currency.
2. (B) Indices where 1970 = 100 if not otherwise indicated.
3. 1972 = 100.
4. Indices for hourly wage.
5. 1971 = 100.
6. 1973 = 100.

Sources: ILO, *Yearbook of Labour Statistics* (1978, 1979); *Statistical Yearbook of the Republic of China* (1979); *Korea Statistical Yearbook* (1980).

average manufacturing worker. Finally, in Taiwan, workers in the textiles and electronics industries have received wage increases below the average for manufacturing workers.

In short, we can characterise the increases in manufacturing wages to the NICs as a development that has given workers increased real wages, although, as a rule, the different manufacturing industries have maintained their relative positions with respect to the wages paid.

Before concluding this section, it should be noted that the growth of real wages during the 1970s has not made the cheap labour argument of protectionism less frequent. As shown by Table 3.2, the differences between wage costs in the 'old' industrial countries and in the NICs are still considerable.

Table 3.2: Estimated Hourly Compensation for Production Workers in Manufacturing, 1979[1,2]

	US Dollars	Index (USA = 100)	
Brazil	1.73	19	(18)[3]
Mexico[4]	2.31	25	(30)
Hong Kong[5]	1.25	14	(11)
Singapore	1.09	12	(12)
South Korea	1.11	12	(6)
Taiwan	1.01	11	(8)
Japan	5.59	62	(48)
Sweden	11.33	125	(113)
USA	9.06	100	(100)

Notes:

1. Preliminary estimates prepared by the US Department of Labor, Bureau of Labor Statistics (1981).
2. Hourly compensation includes all direct payments made to the worker before payroll deductions of any kind, plus employer expenditures for legally-required insurance programmes and contractual and private plans for the benefit of employees. In addition, compensation includes other taxes on payrolls or employment. Hourly compensation does not include costs of recruitment and training, and plant facilities and services.
3. Indices within parentheses refer to 1975. For years prior to 1975, comparable estimates are not available for NICs.
4. Average of selected manufacturing industries.
5. Overtime pay and shift differentials not included.

In this chapter, without going into the cheap labour debate, we will examine social clauses as one means of raising wages in the manufacturing industries in countries where wages now are so low that the cheap labour argument has a real effect on trade policy formation in the old industrial world.

Economic Effects of a Social Clause on Wages

Once a social clause on wages is incorporated in trade policy, countries with a manufacturing export industry that pays wages below a specified minimum level are assumed to set up a minimum wage law in order to raise wage levels in that industry. If such a law is not established, it is assumed that the country will meet traditional trade barriers in the international market for the commodity concerned. The question then arises as to what the effects on the economy would be, assuming that export economies, that do not satisfy the requirements stated in the clause, enforce a minimum wage law for the manufacturing industry and endeavour to make this law efficient.[18]

Effects in a Full Employment Economy. As has been described in section 3.2, our analysis will be divided into two parts: a short run analysis and an analysis of the economy's adjustment towards a new long run equilibrium. In order to analyse the effects of a sectoral minimum wage that only covers manufacturing industry, we replace equation (12) in the system of equations that relates to the full employment type of economy with

$$dw_M = M_L dp_M + p_M M_{LL} dL_M + p_M M_{LK} dK_M \tag{26}$$

where

dw_M is an exogenous variable.

Due to the introduction of a sectoral minimum wage law for the manufacturing industry, the initial long run equilibrium will be disturbed. In the short run, the allocation of capital is fixed, that is $dK_M = 0$. By solving the equations (13)–(16), (18) and (26), i.e. the system of equations that relates to full employment economies, for an exogenous change in the manufacturing real wage, w_M, we obtain the results presented in Table 3.3.

When the minimum wage is enforced, wages have to be raised in manufacturing. At given commodity prices and unchanged technology, the impact effect will be a lower level of employment and production in this sector. To maintain full employment, the wage level outside manufacturing must fall. Thereby the producers in the rest of the economy will increase their labour force and production. The increased use of labour in agriculture will result in increasing returns to land.

Table 3.3: Short Run Effects of a Social Clause on Wages in a Full Employment Economy

$$dL_M/dw_M = 1/(p_M M_{LL}) < 0$$
$$dL_E/dw_M = A_{LL}/D > 0$$
$$dL_A/dw_M = p_E E_{LL}/D > 0$$
$$dr_M/dw_M = M_{LK}/M_{LL} < 0$$
$$dr_E/dw_M = p_E E_{LK} A_{LL}/D > 0$$
$$dw/dw_M = A_{LL}\,(dL_A/dw_M) < 0$$
$$dv/dw_M = A_{RL}\,(dL_A/dw_M) > 0$$
$$\text{where } D = -p_M M_{LL}(p_E E_{LL} + A_{LL}) < 0$$

Furthermore, since capital is immobile in the short run, the employment effects will give rise to a difference in the marginal return to capital between the two capital-using sectors of the economy. As employment has decreased in manufacturing, we can conclude from the assumptions that were made about the production functions that the marginal productivity of capital has decreased as well. Hence the marginal return to capital has also been negatively affected in the short run. As the reverse sequence of events has taken place in the extractive industry, we may conclude that the marginal return to capital used in this industry has increased. The difference in the returns to capital will induce capital movements from the manufacturing to the extractive industry.

Taking the new short run equilibrium as a point of departure, Table 3.4 describes how each endogenous variable will change along with the reallocation of capital. During this long run adjustment, the manufacturing wage level is kept constant at the stated minimum wage level.

When the capital is moved out of manufacturing and into the extractive industry, the marginal productivity of labour falls in the manufacturing industry and increases in the extractive industry. Consequently, production will fall and more labour will be released from manufacturing during the adjustment process. In fact, labour will leave manufacturing in the same proportion as capital. The reason is that given constant commodity prices, constant returns to scale and the stated minimum wage, the profit maximising producers in the manufacturing industry have already in the short run adjusted the capital–labour ratio to a cost-minimising level. Since the wage level is fixed in manufacturing, there are no incentives to change the short run capital–labour ratio during the process of adjustment. Consequently, the marginal return to capital will also be unchanged.

Table 3.4: The Adjustment Process in a Full Employment Economy with a Sectoral Minimum Wage

$$dL_M/dK_M = L_M/K_M > 0$$

$$dL_E/dK_M = (1/D)M_{KL}(p_E E_{KL} K_M/L_M - A_{LL}) < 0$$

$$dL_A/dK_M = (1/D)p_E M_{KL}[(K_E/L_E - K_M/L_M)E_{KL} - (\theta_E - 1)E_L/L_E] < 0 \quad \text{if } K_M/L_M \leqq K_E/L_E$$

$$dK_E/dK_M = -1$$

$$dw/dK_M = A_{LL}(dL_A/dK_M) > 0 \quad \text{if } K_M/L_M \leqq K_E/L_E$$

$$dv/dK_M = A_{RL}(dL_A/dK_M) < 0 \quad \text{if } K_M/L_M \leqq K_E/L_E$$

$$dr_M/dK_M = 0$$

$$dr_E/dK_M = (1/D)p_E\{p_E M_{LL}(E_{LL}E_{KK} - E^2_{LK}) + A_{LL}M_{KL}[(K_M/L_M - K_E/L_E)E_{LK}L_E/K_E - ((\theta_E - 1)E_K/K_E)(K_M/L_M)]\} > 0 \quad \text{if } K_M/L_M \geqq K_E/L_E$$

where

$$D = -M_{LL}(p_E E_{LL} + A_{LL}) < 0$$

and θ_E is the degree of homogeneity of the production function for the extractive industry. Since we have assumed that the extractive industry displays decreasing returns to scale, $\theta_E < 1$.

From our assumptions regarding the production function for the extractive industry, it follows that $E_{LL}E_{KK} - E^2_{LK} > 0$.

Turning to the adjustment effects on the extractive industry, we note that the increased use of capital gives rise to an increased demand for labour. As long as the extractive industry is more capital-intensive than the manufacturing industry, the wage level prevailing outside the manufacturing sector will fall. This can be explained by the fact that during the process of adjustment, capital and labour will leave manufacturing in fixed proportions. Even if the marginal productivity of labour increases in the extractive industry as a result of the increased use of capital, all the labour that has left the manufacturing industry cannot be employed in this industry if the wage rate is not reduced. Furthermore, there is no incentive for agriculture to increase its demand for labour. Consequently, the non-manufacturing wage must fall. As a result, the agricultural sector will also employ more labour and increase its production. Thereby, the land rent will increase as well.

As concerns the total long run effect on the marginal return to capital, this must be negative and equal to the short run reduction in the marginal return to capital used in manufacturing, unless the clause gives rise to complete industrial specialisation. This means that to avoid complete industrial specialisation, the return to capital used in the extractive industry must fall along with the reallocation of capital, i.e. $dr_E/dK_M > 0$. According to Table 3.4, this will certainly happen if manufacturing is the capital-intensive industry. However, even in the case of a labour-intensive manufacturing industry, as we have assumed in section 3.2, dr_E/dK_M can still be positive. The smaller the difference in capital intensities and the greater the degree of decreasing returns to scale in the extractive industry, the stronger is the tendency for the marginal return to capital to fall in this industry when capital is reallocated.

Effects in a Labour Surplus Economy. Let us now turn to the effects of a social clause on wages in the case of an export economy characterised by a labour surplus. Table 3.5 provides the mathematical expressions for the short run effects. These effects have been derived from the system of equations, describing equilibrium in a labour surplus economy, found in section 3.2.

Table 3.5: Short Run Effects of a Social Clause on Wages in a Labour Surplus Economy

$$dL_M/dw_M = 1/(p_M M_{LL}) < 0$$
$$dr_M/dw_M = M_{LK}/M_{LL} < 0$$
$$dL_E/dw_M = dL_A/dw_M = dw/dw_M = dv/dw_M = dr_E/dw_M = 0$$

In the same way as in the case of a full employment economy, the impact effects of an effective minimum wage law directed against the manufacturing industry are those of reduced employment and production in this part of the economy. In fact, in the short run, these are the only effects on the allocation of resources, since capital is immobile between the sectors and both the non-manufacturing wage level and the commodity prices are fixed. Consequently, a decrease in employment in manufacturing will also give rise to a decrease in the total employment level of the three formal sectors of the economy.

As the use of labour decreases in manufacturing, the marginal productivity of capital, and thereby the return to this factor will also decrease in this industry. Regarding the return to capital used in the extractive industry, and the return to land, we note that these are unaffected in the short run since, in the labour surplus economy, there is no labour market connection between the different sectors of production.

Due to the short run effects on the return to capital in manufacturing, capital will, in the longer run, be moved out of this sector and into the extractive industry. By the same line of reasoning as in the case of adjustment in a full employment economy, the marginal return to capital in manufacturing will be unaffected by the reallocation of capital. Consequently, when capital moves out of manufacturing, labour will also be released, which will maintain the cost minimising capital–labour ratio that has been established already in the short run.

Table 3.6: The Adjustment Process in a Labour Surplus Economy with a Sectoral Minimum Wage

$$dL_M/dK_M = L_M/K_M > 0$$
$$dL_E/dK_M = E_{KL}/E_{LL} < 0$$
$$dr_M/dK_M = 0$$
$$dr_E/dK_M = -(1/E_{LL})p_E(E_{LL}E_{KK} - E^2_{LK}) > 0$$
$$dK_E/dK_M = -1$$
$$dL_A/dK_M = 0$$
$$dL/dK_M = [L_M/(E_{LL}K_M)][(\theta_E - 1)E_L/L_E + (K_M/L_M - K_E/L_E)E_{KL}] > 0 \quad \text{if } K_M/L_M \leqq K_E/L_E$$
$$dw/dK_M = dw_M/dK_M = dv/dK_M = 0$$

Since the non-manufacturing real wage and commodity prices are unaffected by the minimum wage law in question and as the extractive industry has been assumed to display decreasing returns to scale, the marginal return to capital used in this industry will decrease when the use of capital increases. Furthermore, due to the increased use of capital, the marginal productivity of labour will increase as well. Consequently, employment will increase in the extractive industry. However, if manufacturing is the labour-intensive industry, the increased employment in the extractive industry will not outweigh the lower level of employment in manufacturing. Furthermore, as both wages and commodity prices are assumed to be fixed in this type of economy, there are no incentives for agriculture to increase production and employment. Consequently, with manufacturing being the labour-intensive industry, total employment in the three formal sectors of the economy will be reduced. In the case when manufacturing is the capital-intensive industry, we cannot come to any clear-cut conclusions concerning the effects on total employment.

Summary. When a social clause on wages is incorporated in the rules that govern international trade, the impact effect on manufacturing employment, production and thereby also on the return to capital used in this industry, will be negative in economies that are compelled to raise the manufacturing wage level in order to satisfy the requirements of the clause. In the case of labour surplus economies, there will be no other impact effects whereas in full employment economies the real wage paid to non-manufacturing workers must decrease in order to keep the labour force fully employed. Consequently, employment and production in agriculture and the extractive industry will increase in the short run. Due to the expansion of the extractive industry there will be an increase in the return to capital used in this industry. Therefore, we may conclude that in full employment as well as in labour surplus economies there will be a negative short run difference in the returns to capital between manufacturing and the extractive industry.

Due to this difference, capital will be reallocated in the longer run from manufacturing to the extractive industry. In labour surplus economies, this reallocation will enlarge the impact effect on manufacturing employment and production. When capital is reallocated, the extractive industry will expand whereas agriculture will remain unaffected. It has also been found that unless manufacturing is the capital-intensive industry, total employment will be negatively affected by this type of clause. In other cases the employment effect will be indeterminate.

In the case of a full employment economy, the impact effects on manufacturing and the extractive industry will also be magnified by the reallocation of capital. With regard to the agricultural sector, there will be a larger positive impact if manufacturing is labour-intensive. If this is not the case, the total long run effect on wages and thereby on the agricultural employment and production will be indeterminate.

As regards factor rewards, we have found that landowners will be unaffected in labour surplus economies and positively affected in full employment economies, unless manufacturing is capital-intensive. As concerns the return to capital, this will be negatively affected in labour surplus economies whereas, in principle, the total long run effect in full employment economies is indeterminate. However, if the clause does not lead to complete industrial specialisation, the effect on the return to capital must also be negative in this type of economy. We have also found that if manufacturing is labour-intensive, the social clause on wages will have negative effects on employment in labour surplus economies whereas non-manufacturing wages will be negatively affected in full employment economies.

Finally, it should be noted that owners of mines will also receive increased incomes following the introduction of a social clause on manufacturing wages. Once production increases in the extractive industry, the increased payments to labour and capital used in this industry will not exhaust the increased value of production since this industry has been assumed to display decreasing returns to scale in labour and capital. Consequently, owners of other factors of production, not included in the production function, in this case the mines, will receive higher incomes as well.

3.4 A Social Clause on Hours of Work

Hours of work have been at the very centre of the debate on international labour standards for more than a hundred years.[19] Hours of work were also the first working condition to be covered by the conventions of the International Labour Organisation.[20]

In this section, we will analyse the economic effects on an economy that has to regulate hours of work in its export industry when a social clause on this specific working condition is incorporated in international trade policy. However, prior to this analysis, we will provide an indication of the present situation in some of the NICs with regard to the hours of work in manufacturing.

The Present State

In any examination of the statistics of hours of work, there are some pitfalls that should be kept in mind. First, as a rule, statistics are derived by dividing the total number of man-hours actually worked or paid for during a certain period of time by the average number of workers on the payroll during the same period. Using this method a higher proportion of part-time work will reduce the average number of hours of work. Secondly, the statistics do not allow for the possibility that the same worker can be employed by several employers. Consequently, hours of work statistics must be interpreted with great care. With these comments in mind we may now look at the situation in some NICs.

We note that the average week worked in manufacturing in the selected NICs is, with only one exception, Mexico, longer than 48 hours, which was the norm stated in the 1919 ILO convention on hours of work. The longest working weeks are in South Korea and Taiwan, whereas the Mexican manufacturing worker works the shortest week of the workers covered by Table 3.7.

Furthermore, we note that, during the 1970s, there have been no substantial reductions in the hours of work in manufacturing in the four NICs in Table 3.7 apart from Taiwan. A comparison of the number of hours worked in the different parts of the manufacturing industry in Table 3.7 shows that workers in the transport equipment industry generally work the longest weeks while workers in the electrical industry work the shortest week. Finally, a comparison of the hours of work in the NICs with the countries representing 'old' industrial countries indicates that there is a significant difference in the hours worked, and that this difference seems to have increased during the 1970s.

Following the incorporation of a social clause on hours of work in the rules governing international trade, a country with a manufacturing export industry in which the number of hours of work is above the stated maximum will be required to regulate the hours of work in that industry if it is to avoid traditional trade barriers in the international market. We now turn to an analysis of the economic effects of regulations regarding hours of work on the export economy concerned.

Table 3.7: Hours of Work (hours/week)

	Mexico[1]		Singapore[1]		South Korea[1]		Taiwan[1,2]		Japan[1]		Sweden[1,2]		USA[3]	
	1970	1977	1970	1979	1970	1979	1970	1979	1970	1979	1970	1977	1970	1979
Manufacturing	44.9	45.5	48.7	48.5	52.3	52.0	52.7	51.1	43.3	40.6	34.8	30.4	39.8	40.2
Textile	42.5	45.9	47.5	47.1	53.1	52.3	52.2	51.1	43.5	41.4	34.3	29.9	39.9	40.3
Clothing	45.6	45.6	47.6 }	47.7	53.9	54.1	–	47.4	42.3	41.1	32.0	30.1	35.3	35.2
Leather	47.4	45.2	– }		49.5	50.6	52.5	47.9	43.3	41.1	33.1	29.5	37.2	36.5
Electronics	–	–	45.6	46.4	49.7	48.9	50.4	49.0	41.6	40.9	33.6	28.5	39.8	40.3
Transport equipment	45.1	44.3	53.7	56.7	50.5	52.9	52.2	51.6	44.5	41.7	35.0	29.7	40.3	41.2

Notes:

1. Hours actually worked.
2. Adjusted from monthly data.
3. Hours paid for.

Source: ILO, *Yearbook of Labour Statistics* (1972, 1980); *Yearbook of Labour Statistics* (1980), Republic of China.

The Economic Effects of a Social Clause on Hours of Work

Effects in a Labour Surplus Economy. When a social clause on hours of work is incorporated in international trade policy, we should note that this will not affect the production and factor prices in export economies that can be characterised as labour surplus economies. The reason is that in such economies, workers will divide their work efforts between working in the 'clause-covered' manufacturing industry and other parts of the economy, including the informal part of the economy. So in this case, the regulation will leave the total work effort devoted to manufacturing unchanged. However, the work will be carried out by a larger number of workers. Consequently, we may conclude that this type of clause will have no protective effects when it is directed against labour surplus economies.

Effects in a Full Employment Economy. With regard to a full employment economy the economic effects of a social clause on hours of work can be divided into two different cases. First, there is the case when the enforced hours of work regulation is linked to the production units in the manufacturing industry in such a way that a worker employed in one manufacturing production unit may not work in that specific unit more than the number of hours stated in the social clause. In this case, there is no restriction placed on the opportunity for the worker to work in other production units. As a result he may work a total number of hours that exceeds the maximum number stated in the clause. In this case, there will be no economic effects of the social clause. The reason is, that when the number of hours of work is maximised in the manufacturing industry, the workers in this industry try to find jobs in other production units. If this process can work completely inside the manufacturing industry, the only effect of the clause will be that each one of the workers will work less hours at each production unit but work at several units so that the total numbers really worked will be the same as the numbers worked before the introduction of the social clause. In the case when the workers in manufacturing have to look for complementary jobs in agriculture and the extractive industry, there will also be no economic effects of the clause. This is due to the fact that the demand of manufacturing workers for jobs in the non-manufacturing sectors will lead to a fall in wages in these sectors at the same time as wages will rise in manufacturing. In order to maintain an unchanged level of incomes, workers in non-manufacturing production units will begin to work in manufacturing. This process of dividing individual workers' efforts between different sectors of the economy will continue until full employment is established at a wage level that is equal throughout the economy. In fact, this wage level will be the same as the wage level before the introduction of the actual social clause, *ceteris paribus*.

In the second case, the hours of work regulation is designed in such a way that workers employed in the manufacturing industry are not allowed to work outside the production unit where they are employed, as long as this employment relation exists. If efficient, the incorporation of a clause on hours of work will give rise to a wage differential in favour of workers employed in manufacturing. The regulation of hours of work at a constant hourly wage will induce workers to leave their employment and to seek work in other parts of the economy where the hours of work regulation does not exist. As a consequence, wages outside manufacturing will fall in relation to wages paid in manufacturing. A wage differential will arise since in this case there is no possibility to divide the work effort between manufacturing and work in agriculture or the extractive industry, in the way described above. Furthermore, this will affect the overall allocation of resources in the economy. These effects can be analysed within the analytical model presented in section 3.2.

Table 3.8: Short Run Effects of a Wage Differential in a Full Employment Economy (initially $\alpha = 1$)

$$dL_M/d\alpha = -(1/D)(p_E E_{LL} + A_{LL})w < 0$$
$$dL_E/d\alpha = (1/D)A_{LL}w > 0$$
$$dL_A/d\alpha = (1/D)p_E E_{LL}w > 0$$
$$dw/d\alpha = A_{LL}(dL_A/d\alpha) < 0$$
$$dr_M/d\alpha = -(1/D)p_M M_{LK}(p_E E_{LL} + A_{LL})w < 0$$
$$dr_E/d\alpha = (1/D)p_E E_{LK} A_{LL}w > 0$$
$$dv/d\alpha = A_{RL}(dL_A/d\alpha) > 0$$

where

$$D = -[p_M M_{LL}(p_E E_{LL} + A_{LL}) + \alpha p_E E_{LL} A_{LL}] < 0$$

In conformity with the analysis of a social clause on wages, we begin by looking at the short run effects. The mathematical expressions for the short run effects of a wage differential are given in Table 3.8.

When a wage differential in favour of workers in manufacturing arises, the use of labour in this sector will be reduced. To maintain full employment in the economy, the non-manufacturing wage must fall. It should be noted that the fall in the non-manufacturing wage can never be of such a magnitude in the short run that the remaining workers in manufacturing become worse off with respect to their hourly wage.

Table 3.9: The Adjustment Process in a Full Employment Economy with a Wage Differential

$$dL_M/dK_M = (1/D)\,[p_M M_{KL}(p_E E_{LL} + A_{LL}) + p_E E_{KL} A_{LL}\alpha] > 0$$

$$dL_E/dK_M = -(1/D)\,[p_E E_{KL}(p_M M_{LL} + \alpha A_{LL}) + p_M M_{KL} A_{LL}] < 0$$

$$dL_A/dK_M = (1/D)\,p_M p_E M_{KL}[(K_E/L_E - K_M/L_M)E_{KL} - (\theta_E - 1)E_L/L_E] < 0 \quad \text{if } K_M/L_M \leqq K_E/L_E$$

$$dK_E/dK_M = -1$$

$$dw/dK_M = A_{LL}(dL_A/dK_M) > 0 \quad \text{if } K_M/L_M \leqq K_E/L_M$$

$$dv/dK_M = A_{RL}(dL_A/dK_M) < 0 \quad \text{if } K_M/L_M \leqq K_E/L_E$$

$$dr_M/dK_M = (1/D)\,p_M p_E A_{LL} M_{KL}\alpha(L_M/K_M)[(\theta_E - 1)E_L/L_E - (K_E/L_E - K_M/L_M)E_{KL}] < 0 \quad \text{if } K_M/L_M \leqq K_E/L_E$$

$$dr_E/dK_M = (1/D)\,p_E\{p_E(p_M M_{LL} + \alpha A_{LL})(E_{LL}E_{KK} - E^2_{LK}) + p_M A_{LL} M_{KL}(K_M/L_M)[(K_M/L_M - K_E/L_E)(L_M L_E/(K_M K_E))E_{KL} - (\theta_E - 1)E_K/K_E]\}$$

$$dr_E/dK_M - dr_M/dK_M = (1/D)\,p_E\{p_M A_{LL} M_{KL}[(K_E/L_E - K_M/L_M)(\alpha K_E/L_E - K_M/L_M)(L_E L_M/(K_E K_M))E_{KL} - (\theta_E - 1)(\alpha E_L L_M/(L_E K_M) + E_K K_M/(K_E L_M))] + p_E(p_M M_{LL} + \alpha A_{LL})(E_{LL}E_{KK} - E^2_{LK})\} > 0 \quad \text{if } \alpha \geqq 1 \text{ and } K_M/L_M \leqq K_E/L_E$$

where

D is identical to D in Table 3.8, $D < 0$

The return to capital in manufacturing will be lower than the return to capital in the extractive industry, since the allocation of capital is fixed in the short run. This can be explained by the short run reallocation of labour that occurs as a result of the wage differential. The fall in manufacturing employment gives rise to a corresponding decline in the marginal productivity of capital and thereby also in the return to capital. In the same way, the increased use of labour in the extractive industry will give rise to an increased return to capital used in this sector. In the longer run, capital will move out of manufacturing and into the extractive industry in response to this difference in the return to capital. This process of adjustment is mathematically described in Table 3.9.

As the use of capital decreases in manufacturing, labour will be released from this industry. Given that manufacturing is the labour-intensive industry, the percentage release of labour will be lower than that of capital. This can be explained by the fact that the use of labour in manufacturing has already been adjusted in the short run with respect to the changes in working conditions in this industry. Wages and employment in the non-manufacturing sectors of the economy have also been subject to a short run adjustment. Therefore, in the longer run, the transfer of capital from the manufacturing to the extractive industry will increase the latter's demand for labour. At constant factor prices during the process of adjustment, there will be a proportionally equal release of labour and capital from the manufacturing industry. However, as long as the extractive industry has a higher capital–labour ratio than manufacturing, there will be an excess supply of labour at the given wage. Consequently, the wage level must fall in order to maintain full employment. At this lower level of wages, the release of labour from manufacturing will be reduced. Consequently, a lower percentage of labour than of capital will be transferred from this industry.

The return to capital will increase in the manufacturing sector due to the reduced capital–labour ratio. This conclusion is dependent on the assumption of a linear homogeneous production function in manufacturing, which means that the marginal productivities depend critically on the factor intensities, i.e. the lower the capital–labour ratio, the higher the marginal productivity of capital. The effect of the adjustment on the return to capital used in the extractive industry is indeterminate. On the one hand, the return to capital tends to increase as in the manufacturing industry. On the other hand, decreasing returns to scale in the extractive industry means that the expansion in production will exert a downward pressure on the return to capital in this industry. However, a comparison of the expressions for the changes in the returns to capital in the two industries indicates that, given the assumption that manufacturing is labour-intensive, the difference in the returns to capital will decrease along with the reallocation of capital. By solving the equations (12)–(18) for the total long run effects of the introduction of a wage differential, we find

$$dr/d\alpha = (1/D)wp_M M_{LK}\{p_E(E_{LL}E_{KK} - E^2_{LK}) + A_{LL}[E_{LK}(L_M/K_M - L_E/K_E) + (\theta_E - 1)E_K/K_E]\} \quad (27)$$

where

$$D = p_E(E_{LL}E_{KK} - E^2_{LK})(p_M M_{LL} + A_{LL}) + p_M A_{LL}(M_{LL}E_{KK} + M_{KK}E_{LL} - 2M_{LK}E_{LK}) < 0$$

Hence, the total long run effect on the return to capital is negative, given that manufacturing is the capital-intensive industry. On the other hand, if manufacturing is labour-intensive, which is the condition for determinacy with regard to the adjustment effects on real wages and non-manufacturing employment and production, the total long run effect on the return to capital is indeterminate. However, we note that the likelihood of a positive effect increases with the magnitude of the difference in the capital–labour ratio between the extractive and the manufacturing industry.

Finally, due to the reallocation of capital and labour, the incomes for mineowners and the return to land will increase during the process of adjustment. This can be explained by the increased use of capital and labour in the extractive industry and the increased use of labour in agriculture.[21]

Summary. The effects on the production and factor prices of the incorporation of a social clause on hours of work in the rules governing international trade is very uncertain. We have noted that there will be no such effects in export economies that can be characterised as labour surplus economies. Moreover, in the case of full employment economies, this conclusion would also seem plausible. However, the clause will give rise to economic effects if the hours of work regulation is linked to the individual workers employed in manufacturing. In this case a wage differential in favour of manufacturing workers will arise.

The impact effects of such a wage differential are lower manufacturing production and increased production in the other sectors of the economy. Furthermore, real wages will increase in manufacturing and decrease for workers employed outside this industry. Due to the short run reallocation of labour there will be an increase in the incomes for owners of land and mines. The return to capital will tend to increase in the extractive industry and fall in manufacturing. Consequently, in the longer run, capital will be moved out of manufacturing and into the extractive industry. Given that manufacturing is the labour-intensive industry, the short run effects will be enlarged during the process of adjustment. It should be noted here that even though manufacturing workers are never confronted with a lower hourly wage in the short run, this may well be the case when the economy reaches its new long run equilibrium. Finally, as concerns the total long run effect on the return to capital, this will be indeterminate in principle, although we have found that the likelihood of a positive effect increases with the size of the difference in capital intensity between the extractive and the manufacturing industry.

3.5 A Social Clause on Child Labour

Besides hours of work, one of the oldest subjects of discussion in the context of international labour legislation is the existence of child labour. The introduction of a social clause on child labour would mean that countries that use child workers in their export industry would have to cease this practice. If they did not do so their export would be subject to traditional protectionist measures. Before we proceed with an economic analysis of an incorporation of a social clause on child labour in the rules that govern international trade, we will give a brief description of the present state of child labour in different parts of the world.

The Present State

According to a report from the International Labour Organisation in 1979, there were at least 52 million children less than 15 years old working in the world economy at the time of the report.[22] This figure is an estimate, and as such surely an underestimate, based on different national labour statistics. According to Mendelievich, the editor of the report, the number of working children could be expected to be an underestimate since in some countries labour statistics simply exclude all persons below 15 years of age. Furthermore, children who combine school attendance with work are usually excluded from the statistics. A third factor that Mendelievich advances is that the statistics often only deal with children having permanent jobs. Finally, Mendelievich also mentions a very important argument for assuming that the estimate is far too low, namely that child labour is illegal. Therefore, there are strong motives for hiding this type of labour both in reality and in statistics. However, as no more reliable information is available, we shall proceed with an analysis of this statistical information keeping the above comments in mind.

In Table 3.10 the distribution of child labour between different parts of the world is described. From this table it is clear that nearly all of the working children are to be found in developing countries. Furthermore, more than 50 per cent of the child workers are in South-east Asia. According to the information given in Table 3.10 we should also note that working children only make up a very small proportion of the total number of children in the world. However, it is important to remember the very substantial shortcomings of the available statistics.[23] Another point to note in Table 3.10 is that a clear majority, or 80 per cent, of the child workers, covered by the statistics, are unpaid family workers. Finally, it should be observed that even if the number of working children has declined as a percentage of the total number of children, the absolute number of registered child workers has increased during the last three decades.

In most countries there are laws on the minimum age of workers. As a rule, this age varies from 12 to 15 years. Furthermore, the minimum age does not only vary from country to country but also varies inside the countries, with respect to the type of work the children are allowed to perform. For instance, the minimum age for industrial work is normally higher than for other types of work. Nevertheless, in many developing countries children do work in industry. By studying the situation in some specific countries, we can obtain some information on the sectoral distribution of child labour. In Table 3.11, we present statistics on the situation prevailing in Greece, Hong Kong, India and Peru.[24] From the information given in this table, we note that child labour is most frequent in rural areas, where the children are working in agriculture or related sectors of production. In all countries

Table 3.10: Working Children Less than 15 Years Old

Region	1950		1960		1975		1979	
	Total Number of Working Children (millions)	Per cent of Total Number of Children	Total Number of Working Children (millions)	Per cent of Total Number of Children	Total Number of Working Children (millions)	Per cent of Total Number of Children	Total Number of Working Children (millions)	Unpaid family Workers[2] (per cent of total child labour)
World[1]	42.8	4.9	45.2	4.1	54.7	3.8	52.0	80
More developed regions	5.0	2.1	4.1	1.4	1.5	0.5		
Less developed regions	37.7	6.0	41.1	5.1	53.2	4.6		
South Asia	21.2	8.0	30.0	6.8	}40.5	}4.7	29.0	80
East Asia	8.4	3.5	8.3	2.9			9.1	70
Africa	5.8	6.3	6.1	5.2	9.6	5.4	9.7	95
Latin America	2.8	4.3	3.2	3.6	3.3	2.4	3.1	65
Europe	3.0	3.0	2.1	1.9	0.8	0.7	0.7	50
USSR	1.3	2.5	1.3	2.0	–	–	–	–
North America	0.2	0.5	0.3	0.5	0.4	0.6	0.3	10
Oceania	0.04	1.2	0.03	0.7	0.1	2.2	0.1	85

Notes:

1. For 1950 and 1960 Micronesia and Polynesia are excluded (estimated total population 1960: 860,000).
2. Includes a very small number of persons working on their own account.

Sources: For 1950, 1960, ILO, *Year Book of Labour Statistics* (1970), pp. 10–20; 1975, ILO, *Year Book of Labour Statistics* (1978), pp. 16–47; 1979, E. Mendelievich (ed.), *Children at Work* (Geneva, 1979), p. 28.

Table 3.11: Child Labour in Greece, Hong Kong, India and Peru

Sector	Greece 1977 (10–14 years)		Hong Kong 1971 (10–14 years)		India 1971 (0–14 years)		Peru 1972 (6–14 years)	
	Number	Per cent[1]	Number	Per cent[1]	Number[2]	Per cent[1]	Number	Per cent[1]
Agriculture, forestry, fishing, hunting	35,396	54.36	2,380	6.62	9,343	87.01	45,989	56.97
Mining, quarrying, saltworks	200	0.31	2,018	5.62	23	0.21	215	0.27
Manufacturing: total	16,264	24.98	23,690	65.94	654	6.09	3,969	4.92
Textile			(12,449)	(34.65)				
Chemicals, metal, plastic			(7,894)	(21.97)				
Others			(3,347)	(9.32)				
Construction	4,336	6.66	3,915	10.90	59	0.55	730	0.90
Trade, commerce, transport, services	6,608	10.15	3,877	10.79	254	2.37	26,597	32.95
Others	2,308	3.54	45	0.13	405	3.77	3,224	3.99
Total	65,112	100.00	35,925	100.00	10,738	100.00	80,724	100.00

Notes:

1. Per cent of the total number of working children.
2. Thousands.

Source: See note 24.

represented in Table 3.11, apart from Hong Kong, more than 50 per cent of the working children are engaged in such activities. We also note that many of the working children are employed in the service sectors. Of course, this circumstance is closely related to the process of urbanisation that is taking place in many developing countries. When the adults of large size families that move to the cities fail to obtain permanent employment, children as well as the adults have to try to find activities that keep them from starvation. Regarding child labour in the large cities of the developing countries, it can be expected that services including trade, commerce and transport employ the greater part of the working children.

In Hong Kong, which is a highly industrialised city state, the activities in the agricultural sector only employ a minor part of the total economically active population. This is also reflected in the sectoral distribution of the working children. In 1971, most child workers in Hong Kong were employed in the textile manufacturing industry. In Greece, which like Hong Kong can be classified as a relatively industrialised country, a large proportion of the working children also work in manufacturing. However, in the other countries covered by Table 3.11, we note that the manufacturing industry only employs a minor part, 4–6 per cent, of the total number of child workers.

Economic Effects of a Social Clause on Child Labour

As was the case with the previously analysed social clauses, a clause on child labour is assumed to be limited to the manufacturing industry. The incorporation of this type of social clause in the rules governing international trade means that the use of child labour is assumed to be prohibited in manufacturing. What will the economic effects be on the export economies concerned if we assume that they change their legislation in order to satisfy the clause? As has already been indicated, only a small proportion of working children can be generally found in the manufacturing industry. Consequently, it can be expected that the effect of the limited prohibition laid down in the social clause will be to encourage the movement of working children from manufacturing to sectors not covered by the prohibition.

In the following analysis, we evaluate child workers in terms of units of adult labour so that one unit of child labour and one unit of adult labour will be perfect substitutes as factors of production.

In equilibrium one unit of child labour will thereby receive the same wage as one unit of adult labour. However it should be noted that this does not mean that a child worker and an adult worker receive the same wage.

The use of the term 'degree of substitution' of the two categories of workers refers to the number of child workers that is required to replace one adult worker without affecting the level of production. In the case when this degree of substitution is the same in all sectors of production, in the absence of regulations, we can expect to find working children in all sectors. However, in the more realistic case, where the degree of substitution differs between the various sectors of production, all working children will be employed in the sector where child workers are closest substitutes for adult workers.

Effects in a Labour Surplus Economy. In a labour surplus economy, a social clause on child labour will leave the production of the formal sectors unaffected. The prohibition of child labour in manufacturing will reduce the use of this type of labour in this industry. As there is a labour surplus in this type of economy, there will be no problem in finding adults who are willing to replace children at the current wage. Consequently, the employment of adults will increase and the employment of child workers will decrease leaving production unaffected. Of course, this type of change can affect the income distribution in a way that is detrimental for large size families.

Effects in a Full Employment Economy. When a social clause on child labour is directed against the manufacturing exports of a full employment economy, the economic effects are more complicated than is the case with the labour surplus type of economy. However, as long as there is adult labour that can replace child labour in manufacturing, which we assume is always the case, and when the degree of substitution between the two categories of workers is the same in all sectors of production, the effects are still very clear-cut. Given these assumptions, the social clause will give rise to a migration of child labour from manufacturing to the non-manufacturing sectors of the economy, and a migration of adult labour in the opposite direction, leaving factor rewards and production unaffected. The prohibition of child labour in manufacturing will lead to the release of child workers from this industry. Since adult labour is assumed to be a perfect substitute for child labour, the demand for adult labour will increase in manufacturing. Consequently, there will be an excess supply of child labour and an excess demand for adult labour at the initial wage. As a result, the wage for child labour will decrease and the wage for adult labour will increase. Since the degree of substitution between the two types of labour has been assumed to be the same in all sectors of production, the non-manufacturing sectors will increase their demand for child workers and release adult labour. As a consequence, the wages of the two types of labour will return to their initial level.

Let us now turn to the case when the degree of substitution between the two categories of labour differs between the sectors of production. In this case, as mentioned above, all working children will be employed in the sector where child workers and adult workers are closest substitutes, given that there is no regulation concerning the allocation of child labour. Therefore, if children work initially in manufacturing, a social clause on child labour will imply a reduction in the available labour force measured in units of adult labour. This is due to the fact that the total number of child workers represents a smaller labour force in terms of adult labour when children are employed in non-manufacturing sectors than was the case prior to the clause, when children worked in manufacturing.

A central theorem in economic analysis of changes in factor endowments is the Rybczynski theorem.[25] According to this theorem, in a two-sector economy at constant commodity prices, a reduction in the labour force will give rise to a lower level of production in the labour intensive sector and increased production in the capital-intensive part of the economy, without affecting factor prices.

One critical assumption for the original derivation of this theorem was that production functions displayed constant returns to scale. As described in section 3.2, our analysis concerns economies with three sectors of production where one of the capital-using sectors displays decreasing returns to scale in labour and capital. Therefore, the Rybczynski theorem cannot be applied directly to our case. However, the assumed form of the agricultural production function makes it possible to concentrate on the two capital-using sectors. Furthermore, by assuming that the extractive industry, which displays decreasing returns to scale, is the capital-intensive industry, the Rybczynski theorem can be demonstrated to carry over as concerns the production effects in the two capital-using sectors in the economy.[26] However, factor prices will now be affected since one of the industries displays decreasing returns to scale.

By solving the system of equations for the full employment economy, derived in section 3.2, for exogenous changes in the labour force keeping the allocation of capital unchanged, we obtain the short run effects presented in Table 3.12.

Table 3.12: Short Run Effects of a Social Clause on Child Labour in a Full Employment Economy

$$dL_M/dL = (1/D)p_E E_{LL} A_{LL} > 0$$
$$dL_E/dL = (1/D)p_M M_{LL} A_{LL} > 0$$
$$dL_A/dL = (1/D)p_M p_E M_{LL} E_{LL} > 0$$
$$dw/dL = A_{LL}(dL_A/dL) < 0$$
$$dv/dL = A_{RL}(dL_A/dL) > 0$$
$$dr_M/dL = (1/D)p_M p_E M_{LK} E_{LL} A_{LL} > 0$$
$$dr_E/dL = (1/D)\, p_M p_E M_{LL} E_{LK} A_{LL} > 0$$
$$dr_M/dL - dr_E/dL = (1/D)p_M p_E M_{LK} A_{LL}[(K_M/L_M - K_E/L_E)E_{LK} + (\theta_E - 1)E_L/L_E] > 0 \quad \text{if } K_M/L_M \leqq K_E/L_E$$

where $D = p_M p_E M_{LL} E_{LL} + p_M M_{LL} A_{LL} + p_E E_{LL} A_{LL} > 0$

We find that in the short run, employment, measured as the number of units of adult labour, will fall in all sectors. The reason is that due to the prohibition of child labour in manufacturing, there will be an excess supply of child labour at thc initial wage. Furthermore, in non-manufacturing sectors we have now assumed that more child workers are required to replace one adult worker than was the case in manufacturing. Therefore, after evaluating child labour in terms of units of adult labour, the net effect will be an excess demand for labour at the initial wage. As a result, wages will increase and employment will decrease in all sectors of production.

Due to the lower level of employment, the returns to other factors of production will be reduced as well. In the short run, the returns to capital will fall in the two industrial sectors. It will decline most in manufacturing, which has been assumed to be the labour-intensive industry. However, if manufacturing is the capital-intensive industry we cannot come to any clear-cut conclusions regarding which industry has experienced the greatest decline in the return to capital, since, in this case, the labour-intensive industry displays decreasing returns to scale.

Assuming that manufacturing is labour-intensive, capital will be reallocated from this industry to the extractive industry. The reallocation of labour and the change in factor prices in response to this reallocation of capital has already been described and analysed in conjunction with the analysis of a social clause on hours of work (see Table 3.9).[27] On the basis of that analysis we conclude that the short run effects on manufacturing employment and production will be enlarged and that the real wage will be negatively affected by the capital reallocation. However, it should be noted that this negative influence on wages can never outweigh the positive impact effect.[28] Therefore, even if agricultural employment and production increase as a result of the reallocation of capital, the total long run effect of a social clause on child labour will be negative for this part of the economy.

With regard to the extractive industry, employment and production will increase as more capital is allocated to the industry. Furthermore, the total long run effect on capital of the reduction in the labour force will be negative.

$$dr/dL = (1/D)p_E p_M M_{LK} A_{LL}(E_{LL}E_{KK} - E^2_{LK}) > 0 \qquad (28)$$

where

D is identical to D in (27), $D < 0$[29]

It can be concluded from the total long run effects on the real wage level and the return to capital, that there will be a total long run reduction in unit costs of production in the extractive industry. At constant commodity prices, this means that there will be an incentive for this industry to expand its production until the unit costs of production equal the price of the commodity produced. So, even though, in the short run, the social clause on child labour negatively affects the extractive production, and thereby the income of mineowners, the positive effects that arise out of the reallocation of capital will make the total long run effects on this industry positive.[30]

Summary. When a social clause on child labour is incorporated in the rules that govern international trade, it is very doubtful whether this will give rise to any effects on the production and factor prices in export economies where children work in the manufacturing export industry. We have found that there will be no such effects in export economies that can be characterised as labour surplus economies. Nevertheless, we should note that income distribution in this type of economy may well be affected in a way that is detrimental to large size families.

In the case when the export economies concerned can be characterised as full employment economies, we must distinguish between two cases. First, if the degree of substitution between child workers and adult workers is the same in all sectors of the economy, there will be no effects on production, factor prices and income distribution. However, if the degree of substitution of the two categories of labour differs between the sectors of production, the prohibition of child labour in manufacturing will give rise to a reduction in the available labour force, measured as units of adult labour. As a result of the reduction in the labour force, and the accompanying increase in the real wage, all sectors will be negatively affected in the short run. In the longer run, given that manufacturing is labour-intensive, capital will be reallocated from manufacturing into the extractive industry. As a consequence, factor prices and production will change and the negative impact effect on manufacturing production will be enlarged whereas the impact effect on agricultural production will be counteracted but not outweighed. Finally, in relation to the extractive industry, the positive effects on production that follow from the reallocation of capital will more than outweigh the negative impact effect.

Regarding factor rewards, we have found that owners of capital and land will receive lower earnings, whereas owners of mines will increase their earnings following an expansion of the extractive production. The wages of adult workers will increase whereas children will receive lower incomes from their work. Consequently, in the case of a full employment economy a clause on child labour may also be unfavourable for large size families.

3.6 A Social Clause on Occupational Health and Safety

As was the case with the question of international legislation on hours of work and child labour, the question of incorporating rules on occupational health and safety in a set of international labour standards also has a century-long history. In Chapter 1 we noted that as early as 1876, at an international congress of hygiene held in Brussels, the central role of hygiene at work in international labour legislation was given considerable emphasis. Furthermore, we should not forget the 1906 Berne Convention on the use of white phosphorus. One hundred years or so after the congress in Brussels, the question of incorporating standards on occupational health and safety in a set of labour standards in trade policy has been strongly advocated. The documents on international labour standards and trade, that have been worked out by the US and Canadian Departments of Labour, provide clear examples of the central place of occupational health and safety.[31] The Swedish trade union movement has also given considerable priority to the role of occupational health and safety standards in the demands for social clauses.[32]

In the debate on the demands for incorporating standards on occupational health and safety in international trade laws, references are often made to the same type of arguments that can be found in the Preamble to the Constitution of the ILO, where it is stated that 'the failure of any nation to adopt human conditions of labour is an obstacle in the way of other nations which desire to improve the conditions in their own countries'.[33] As a result of the differences that exist between countries with regard to legislation on occupational health and safety, there is obviously a tendency for unhealthy and dangerous industries to move their activities from countries with high requirements with respect to occupational health and safety to countries where these requirements are low. In this context producers may clearly use occupational health and safety as a means of competition. In order to reduce this type of international competition, international standards on health and safety in working life have been formed and agreed upon since the Berne Convention on white phosphorus. Table 3.13 lists ILO occupational health and safety conventions of interest to manufacturing workers.

From Table 3.13, it is clear that very few countries have ratified conventions on occupational health and safety in the manufacturing industry. Even if this should not be interpreted as a description of the state of health and safety in manufacturing, it indicates that occupational health and safety is a quite recent area of labour market legislation in a majority of countries. With this in mind, we now turn to the situation in some of the newly industrialised developing countries, in order to see whether we can find some support for the argument that the occupational health and safety standards in the manufacturing industry of these countries are very low.

Table 3.13: ILO Conventions on Occupational Health and Safety in Manufacturing

Convention		Number of Ratifications up to July 1981
No. 13	White Lead (Painting) Convention (1921)	52
No. 115	Radiation Protection Convention (1960)	35
No. 119	Guarding of Machinery Convention (1963)	35
No. 127	Maximum Weight Convention (1967)	20
No. 136	Benzene Convention (1971)	24
No. 139	Occupational Cancer Convention (1974)	18
No. 148	Working Environment (Air Pollution, Noise and Vibration) Convention (1977)	10[1]
No. 152	Occupational Safety and Health (Dock Work) Convention (1979)	3
No. 155	Occupational Safety and Health and the Working Environment Convention (1981)	0

Note:
1. Of which two countries have only partially ratified the convention.

Source: Information received from the ILO.

The Present State

To indicate the real world situation of the occupational health and safety standard is very difficult. Here, as well as in the case of other working conditions, laws are of limited interest if one does not have information on how the laws are interpreted. Regarding statistical information on accidents and occupational diseases, severe problems of comparisons between countries exist due to differences in the classification system. Therefore, in accordance with ILO's *Yearbook of Labour Statistics* we have chosen to indicate the situation in some non-European NICs by presenting statistics on fatal accidents in manufacturing. To give some

Table 3.14: Fatal Accidents in Manufacturing in Some NICs and OECD Countries (rate per 1,000,000 man-hours worked)

	1970	1971	1972	1973	1974	1975	1976	1977	1978
Mexico[1,2]	0.08	0.15	0.02	0.14	0.11				
Singapore[3]	0.07	0.05	0.08	0.09	0.11	0.07	0.07	0.04	0.15
South Korea[1,2,4]	0.10	0.10	0.09	0.07	0.10	0.08	0.06	0.07	
Taiwan[1]	0.07	0.08	0.09	0.08	0.10	0.09	0.09	0.09	0.09
Japan[3,4]	0.04	0.03	0.03	0.03	0.02	0.02	0.01	0.02	0.01
Sweden[2]	0.05	0.04	0.04	0.03	0.03	0.03			
USA[3]	0.03	0.04	0.04	0.03	0.03	0.03	0.03		

Notes:

1. The figures given in the statistical sources have been recalculated using the following formula in order to enable comparisons to be made between countries:

$d = c \times 1{,}000/(52 \times \text{average hours of work per week})$, where c = rate per 1,000 persons employed and d = rate per 1,000,000 man hours worked

In the case of Taiwan, c indicates the per cent rate of insurant.

2. Compensated accidents.
3. Reported accidents.
4. In the case of South Korea, only production units with 50 or more workers are included; for Japan, only production units with 100 or more workers are included.

Sources: ILO, *Yearbook of Labour Statistics*; *Yearbook of Labour Statistics*, Republic of China.

indication of the relative standard in NICs and some 'older' industrial countries, Table 3.14 also includes statistics on fatal accidents in Sweden, the United States and Japan.

From Table 3.14 we conclude that the frequency of fatal accidents in the NICs concerned is far above the corresponding level prevailing in the three industrialised countries covered by the table. Consequently, it does not seem too rash to assume that the risks for accidents and diseases in the manufacturing industries of the newly industrialised countries are far above what can be considered acceptable in the traditional industrialised countries.

It is argued that the incorporation of a social clause on occupational health and safety, in the rules that govern international trade, would prevent low standards of this specific type of working condition being used as a means of international competition. Furthermore, it is argued that the existence of such a clause could pave the way for further improvements in the occupational health and safety standards in developed as well as in developing countries.

Economic Effects of a Social Clause on Occupational Health and Safety

In the same way as for social clauses on wages, hours of work and child labour we assume that the incorporation of a clause on occupational health and safety is followed by changes in the working environment in countries with substandard working conditions. Furthermore, we assume that the clause only deals with the occupational health and safety standard in the manufacturing industry which is assumed to produce for export.

To analyse the effects of a clause on occupational health and safety, we must find an answer to the question of how to represent changes in the working environment in the analytical model presented in section 3.2. Since the working environment is given a wide interpretation and since most aspects of the working environment are directly related to the production technique, it seems natural to use a technology parameter to represent the state of the working environment. Therefore, in our model, a change in the working environment, or occupational health and safety, is represented by a technological change. Let us give some examples that support this choice of representation.

One obvious example is when the speed of production is reduced. Sometimes this can clearly be characterised as an improvement in the working environment, and it can always be characterised as a technological change. Another type of change that supports this method of representing changes in the working environment is when floor space is increased in order to give each worker an area above a certain minimum. Another example that can be used in this context is a change in the maximum weights that a worker may lift. Finally, changes in the classification of chemical substances that may be used in production not only imply a change in technology but have also the characteristics of changes in occupational health and safety.

Having decided upon the representation of changes in occupational health and safety in the manufacturing industry we will make some additional comments before proceeding with the analysis of the economic effects of such changes. First, it can be assumed that the actual changes in the working environment can be characterised as a negative technical change, since there has been no economic justification for such changes prior to the introduction of the social clause in question. Furthermore, when we turn to the economic analysis of a social clause on this specific working condition, we will find that the effects are far more complicated than those arising out of clauses on wages, hours of work and child labour. This can be partially explained by the imprecise meaning of a change in occupational health and safety. However, like Hicks, we classify changes in technology, which are interpreted here as changes in the working environment or occupational health and safety, as *neutral* changes, *labour-using* changes and *capital-using* changes.[34]

Neutral changes are characterised by reducing the marginal productivity of capital and labour in equal proportions, whereas *labour-using* changes decrease the marginal productivity of capital proportionally more than the marginal productivity of labour, and the reverse holds for *capital-using* changes of the working environment. It should be noted that the marginal productivity of labour, may well rise in the case of a labour-using improvement of the working environment, whereas the same is true for the marginal productivity of capital in the case of capital-using changes.

In the following analysis, we will also use the concepts of *productivity-decreasing* and *productivity-increasing* changes. *Productivity-decreasing* changes are defined as changes that decrease the marginal productivity of both capital and labour, whereas *productivity-increasing* changes are defined as changes that increase the marginal productivity of either capital or labour. Consequently, productivity-decreasing changes can be neutral, labour-using or capital-using, whereas productivity-increasing changes can only be of the two latter types.

Effects in a Full Employment Economy.

Short Run Effects. When improvements in the working environment are made in the manufacturing industry of a full employment economy, the short run effects depend critically on

Table 3.15: Short Run Effects of a Social Clause on Occupational Health and Safety in a Full Employment Economy

$$dL_M/dt_M = (1/D)p_M(p_E E_{LL} + A_{LL})M_{Lt} \lessgtr 0 \quad \text{as } M_{Lt} \lessgtr 0$$
$$dL_E/dt_M = -(1/D)p_M A_{LL} M_{Lt} \gtrless 0 \quad \text{as } M_{Lt} \lessgtr 0$$
$$dL_A/dt_M = -(1/D)p_M p_E E_{LL} M_{Lt} \gtrless 0 \quad \text{as } M_{Lt} \lessgtr 0$$
$$dw/dt_M = A_{LL}(dL_A/dt_M) \lessgtr 0 \quad \text{as } M_{Lt} \lessgtr 0$$
$$dv/dt_M = A_{RL}(dL_A/dt_M) \gtrless 0 \quad \text{as } M_{Lt} \lessgtr 0$$
$$dr_M/dt_M = (p_M/D)\{p_M(p_E E_{LL} + A_{LL})M_{LK}M_t/L_M - p_E E_{LL} A_{LL} M_{Kt}\} < 0 \quad \text{if } M_{Kt} \leqq 0$$
$$dr_E/dt_M = -(1/D)p_M p_E E_{LK} A_{LL} M_{Lt} \gtrless 0 \quad \text{as } M_{Lt} \lessgtr 0$$
$$dr_M/dt_M - dr_E/dt_M = (1/D)p_M\{p_M(p_E E_{LL} + A_{LL})M_{LK}M_t/L_M + p_E A_{LL}[E_{KL}(M_{Lt} + K_E M_{Kt}/L_E) - (\theta_E - 1)E_L M_{Kt}/L_E]\}$$

where

$$D = -[p_M M_{LL}(p_E E_{LL} + A_{LL}) + p_E E_{LL} A_{LL}] < 0$$

Note:

By employing Euler's theorem on the manufacturing production function $M(L_M, K_M, t_M)$ and differentiating with respect to the technology parameter t_M, we get:

$$M_t = L_M M_{Lt} + K_M M_{Kt}$$

Furthermore $M_t < 0$ according to the assumption that the changes in occupational health and safety standards can be characterised as negative technical changes. We note that according to this assumption, the manufacturing marginal products of the two factors of production cannot both be positively affected by the changes.

By rewriting the above expression as $M_t/L_M = M_{Lt} + (K_M/L_M)M_{Kt} < 0$ we can conclude that if $M_{Kt} \leqq 0$ and $K_M/L_M \leqq K_E/L_E$ then

$$M_{Lt} + (K_E/L_E)M_{Kt} < 0 \text{ as well.}$$

the type of changes that have to be made, or more precisely on the signs of the accompanying changes of the marginal productivities of capital and labour respectively.

In Table 3.15, the mathematical expressions for the short run effects are given. These expressions have been derived as set out in section 3.2.

Productivity-decreasing changes. As long as the required changes are *productivity-decreasing*, the marginal productivity of labour falls in the manufacturing industry. The use of labour thereby decreases in this industry. In order to maintain full employment in the economy at given commodity prices, employment has to increase in the other sectors. For this to happen, the wage must fall.

With respect to the short run effects on the return to capital, we note that capital used in manufacturing will receive a lower return after the changes while capital used in the extractive industry will receive higher returns. This can be explained by the fact that the improvement in the working environment in manufacturing has decreased the marginal productivity of capital and thereby also the return to capital in this sector. This negative effect is strengthened by the reduction in the productivity of capital that comes from the reduced use of labour in manufacturing. In the same way, the increased use of labour in the extractive industry gives rise to an increased marginal productivity of capital and consequently a higher return to capital used in this sector. Thus in the case of productivity-decreasing changes in the working environment in manufacturing, the short run effects on wages will be negative as will the effects on the production and return to capital in manufacturing. The short run effects on non-manufacturing production will be positive. Consequently, the rewards to factors of production not used in the manufacturing industry will be positively affected as well.

Productivity-increasing changes. If the social clause on occupational health and safety demands improvements in the working environment that are labour- or capital-using, we cannot exclude the possibility that the changes may increase the marginal productivity of either labour or capital in manufacturing. If this is the case, the economic effects of the improvements become more complex than otherwise would have been the case.

The short run effects on the use of labour in manufacturing and on the wage level will be in the same direction as the change in the marginal productivity of labour in manufacturing. Consequently, in the case of *labour-using* changes in the manufacturing working environment it is possible that the demand for labour increases in this industry. As the other sectors are not directly affected by the social clause, the wage level will be bid up in this case. Consequently, labour will move from agriculture and the extractive industry to the manufacturing industry. Hence, in the short run, production in non-manufacturing sectors will tend to decrease, whereas the effect on manufacturing production is indeterminate. Furthermore, as less labour is employed in the extractive industry, the marginal productivity of capital and thereby the return to capital will fall. In manufacturing, the increased use of labour will have a positive effect on the marginal productivity of capital. However, in the case of labour-using changes, we know that the marginal productivity of capital is affected negatively. In fact, according to the assumption of negative total productivity change, the negative effect on the marginal productivity of capital must be sufficiently large in the short run to outweigh the positive effect on this productivity that is derived from the increased use of labour. Consequently, the return to capital will decrease also in this industry.

The other type of productivity-increasing changes in the working environment created by a social clause on occupational health and safety, is *capital-using* changes. In this case, it is possible that there is an increase in the marginal productivity of capital used in manufacturing. When the changes of the working environment are capital-using, the marginal productivity of labour always decreases. Consequently, there will be a fall in manufacturing employment. To maintain full employment in the economy, the wage must fall so that the non-manufacturing sectors can increase their employment. From the short run employment effects, we can conclude that production in agriculture and the extractive industry will increase in the short run, whereas the short run effect on manufacturing output must be negative. Regarding the return to capital, we are aware that in manufacturing, the marginal productivity of capital is positively affected by the changes in the working environment. On the other hand, this positive effect will be counteracted by the negative productivity effect that results from the reduced use of labour in this industry. Therefore, in the short run, the effect on the marginal productivity of capital and thereby the return to capital used in manufacturing will be indeterminate. The short run effect on the return to capital used in the extractive industry is clear-cut. Due to the increased use of labour in this industry, the marginal productivity of capital, and thereby also the return to capital, will increase.

Adjustment to a New Long Run Equilibrium. Due to the short run effects on the returns to capital, capital will be reallocated in the longer run. In order to establish the direction of this reallocation, we must determine the sign of the difference between the returns to capital in the capital-using sectors of the economy.

From the short run analysis, we are aware that when the social clause on occupational health and safety gives rise to productivity-decreasing changes in the working environment in the manufacturing sector, the return to capital will decrease in this industry and increase in the extractive industry. Consequently, in the case of productivity-decreasing changes, capital will be reallocated from manufacturing to the extractive industry in the longer run.

Turning to the case of productivity-increasing changes, we also note that in the case of labour-using changes, a negative difference will appear between the return to capital in manufacturing and the return to capital in the extractive industry, given that manufacturing is the labour-intensive industry. Consequently, in this case, capital will also be moved out of manufacturing and into the extractive industry.

With regard to productivity-increasing changes that can be characterised as capital-using, we have found that in the short run, the return to capital may increase in both industries. There is also a possibility that large increases in the marginal productivity of capital will raise the return to capital used in manufacturing by more than was the case for capital used in the extractive industry. If this holds, in the longer run, capital will be reallocated from the extractive industry and into the manufacturing industry.

An examination of the process of adjustment along the economy's path to a new long run equilibrium, shows that this process can be described mathematically using the same expressions as those given in Table 3.9.[35] Referring to this table and the adjoining analysis, we can conclude that in the case when capital is moved out of manufacturing, which is assumed to be the labour-intensive industry, labour will also be released from this industry but at a lower percentage rate than was the case for capital. Given the above assumption, wages will fall and agricultural employment and production, and thereby also land rent, will increase during the process of adjustment to a new long run equilibrium. Furthermore, the increased use of labour and capital in the extractive industry will give rise to increased incomes for mineowners.[36]

As concerns the total long run effect on the return to capital, this is, in principle, indeterminate. However by solving equations (12)–(18) for the long run effect on the return to capital of a technical change in manufacturing we get:

$$dr/dt_M = (1/D)p_M\{p_E(E_{LL}E_{KK} - E^2_{LK}) \times (A_{LL}M_{Kt} - p_M M_{LK}M_t/L_M) - p_M M_{LK}A_{LL}(M_t/L_M) \times [(\theta_E - 1)E_K/K_E + E_{KL}(L_M/K_M - L_E/K_E)]\} \quad (29)$$

where

D is identical to D in (27), $D < 0$.

From this we conclude that, when manufacturing is the labour-intensive industry, the likelihood of a positive long run effect on the return to capital increases with the magnitude of the difference between the capital intensities in the extractive and manufacturing industry, respectively.[37]

Finally, if, in the short run, the social clause on occupational health and safety gives rise to a positive difference between the returns to capital in manufacturing and the extractive industry, capital will be reallocated from the extractive industry to the manufacturing industry in the longer run. When this is the case, the adjustment effects described above will be reversed and the total long run effects of the clause will be indeterminate.

Effects in a Labour Surplus Economy. Compared to the effects of a social clause on occupational health and safety in a full employment economy, the effects of such a clause on a labour surplus economy are very clear-cut. In Table 3.16 the mathematical expressions describing the short run effects are given.

Table 3.16: Short Run Effects of a Social Clause on Occupational Health and Safety in a Labour Surplus Economy

$dL_M/dt_M = -M_{Lt}/M_{LL} \lesseqgtr 0 \quad \text{as } M_{Lt} \lesseqgtr 0$

$dr_M/dt_M = p_M M_t/K_M < 0$

$dL_E/dt_M = dL_A/dt_M = dr_E/dt_M = dv/dt_M = 0$

We note that in this type of economy, only the sector covered by the clause, in this case the manufacturing industry, will be affected in the short run. Furthermore, it is only the effect on the marginal productivity of labour that is decisive for the effects on the resource allocation. Consequently, in the case of neutral or capital-using changes in the working environment in manufacturing, we may conclude that employment will decrease in this industry. Hence, in these cases, the social clause will give rise to a negative short run employment effect in the formal part of the economy. In the case of labour-using changes in the manufacturing working environment, we have noted that the marginal productivity of labour may increase. If so, the employment effects of the clause will be reversed.

Finally, turning to the short run effect on the return to capital in manufacturing, we find that it is negative for all types of changes in the working environment. By the same line of reasoning as in the full employment economy, changes that increase the marginal productivity of labour will give rise to a negative short run effect on the marginal return to capital. In the case of changes that increase the marginal productivity of capital, the short run effect on the return to capital will also be negative. Since wages cannot be changed in this type of economy, the negative effect on the productivity of capital that arises out of the reduced use of labour will always outweigh the positive productivity effect that is directly related to the change in the working environment.

Due to the short run effect on the return to capital in manufacturing, capital will, in the longer run, move out of this industry and into the extractive industry. The economic effects of this reallocation are mathematically described in Table 3.6 in section 3.3. Referring to this table, we find that the reallocation of capital will not affect the return to capital in manufacturing. This can be explained with reference to the constant wage that characterises this type of economy, constant commodity prices and the assumption of constant returns to scale. Consequently, when capital is transferred from manufacturing, labour will also leave this industry thus maintaining the cost-minimising capital–labour ratio, that had already been established in the short run.

When capital is reallocated from manufacturing into the extractive industry, employment in the latter industry will increase. This is due to the assumption that more capital combined with a given labour force implies an increased marginal productivity of labour. However, if manufacturing is the labour-intensive industry, the increased use of labour in the extractive industry cannot outweigh the reduced level of employment in manufacturing. Consequently, in this case, employment in the formal sectors of the economy will fall during the adjustment process. In the case when manufacturing displays the higher capital–labour ratio of the two industries, no clear-cut conclusion can be established for the total employment effects in the three formal sectors. Finally, we should note that the incorporation of a social clause on occupational health and safety in the rules that govern international trade does not affect the agricultural sector in labour surplus economies.

Summary. When a social clause on occupational health and safety is incorporated in the rules that govern international trade, the effects on economies that must change the working environment in their manufacturing industry are more complex than is the case for social clauses on other specific working conditions. However, as long as the necessary changes in the working environment reduce the marginal productivity of labour as well as of capital, the effects will be clear-cut.

The impact effect of productivity-decreasing changes will be lower levels of manufacturing production and employment, and a reduction in the return to capital used in this industry. In labour surplus economies, there will be no other effects in the short run, whereas in full employment economies, the real wage must decrease in order to maintain full employment. Consequently, in this latter type of economy, the impact effect on the extractive industry and agriculture will be positive as will the return to capital used in the extractive industry. Hence, in labour surplus as well as in full employment economies, a social clause that demands productivity-decreasing changes in manufacturing will give rise to a short run difference in the return to capital between the two industries. Due to this difference, in the longer run, capital will be moved out of manufacturing and into the extractive industry.

When capital is reallocated, the short run effect on production will be enlarged in labour surplus economies. This will also be the case in full employment economies as concerns the impact effects on production and factor rewards, with the exception of the return to capital, when manufacturing is the labour-intensive industry. Furthermore, in labour surplus economies, the reallocation of capital will also give rise to a positive effect on the extractive industry and thereby on the incomes of mineowners. Regarding the total long run effect on the return to capital, this will be negative in the case of labour surplus economies, whereas, in principle, it will be indeterminate in full employment economies. However, we have found that the likelihood of a positive effect increases with the magnitude of the difference in capital intensities between the extractive and the manufacturing industry.

Let us now turn to the effects of productivity-increasing changes in the manufacturing working environment, i.e. changes that improve the marginal productivity of either labour or capital. In the case of changes that improve the marginal productivity of capital, the impact effects on production and factor rewards, except in relation to the return to capital in full employment economies, will be in the same direction as in the case of productivity-decreasing changes. In the case of changes that improve the marginal productivity of labour, the impact effect on manufacturing production will be indeterminate whereas the effects on the extractive industry and agriculture in a full employment economy will be negative. Finally, in the case of productivity-increasing changes, the total long run effects on production and factor rewards have been found to be indeterminate in full employment economies. In labour surplus economies, however, the effects will be in the same direction as in the case of productivity-decreasing changes, unless the necessary changes in the working environment increase the marginal productivity of labour. For this type of labour-using changes, the total long run effect on the manufacturing industry will be indeterminate while the effects on the extractive industry will be positive. The effect on the incomes of mineowners will also be positive while the return to capital will decrease.

3.7 Welfare Economic Aspects on Social Clauses on Specific Working Conditions

A central concept in welfare economic theory is *Pareto optimum*. An economy is said to be in a Pareto optimal state when no other feasible state exists that would give one individual a higher level of utility without moving at least one other individual to a lower level of utility.

For a Pareto optimal state to exist the following conditions must be satisfied:

(1) Between any two goods the marginal rate of subjective substitution must be the same for all individuals, and this common rate should also be equal to the marginal rate of technically transforming one of those goods into the other through transferring any factor of production from one of these goods to the other.
(2) For each individual the subjective marginal rate of substitution between any factor of production and a good must be the same; and this common rate should be equal to the marginal technical rate of transformation of that factor into the product in question.[38]

If these conditions are not satisfied, the economy cannot be at a Pareto optimum and one or more *distortions* are said to exist.

In a market economy without any externalities, collective goods or indivisibilities, the conditions above will be satisfied if all producers and all consumers maximise their profits and utilities respectively in relation to the same set of prices. In the case of a small open economy, a Pareto optimum also requires that the domestic rate of transformation should equal the foreign rate of transformation. In other words, the economy should take part in international trade without making any interventions.

In this section, we will analyse the question of initial optimality or inoptimality in economies that have to change their working conditions when social clauses on various specific working conditions are incorporated in the rules that govern international trade. Furthermore, we shall examine the relationship between such clauses and optimality.

In conformity with the rest of this chapter, we assume that there are no trade barriers when the social clauses are introduced. We also retain the assumption that the individual economies concerned take commodity prices as given by the international market.

Before we proceed with the analysis of the relationship between social clauses and optimality, we will comment on the basic distortion that exists in labour surplus economies.

A Basic Distortion in Labour Surplus Economies

Negishi has analysed the question of domestic distortions in a two-sector economy characterised by a labour surplus. He has proved that 'if the marginal productivity of labour in the modern sector is equal to the average productivity of labour in the subsistence sector, there exists a second best tariff superior to free trade'.[39] The reason is that a tariff on imports that competes with the output of the modern sector will normally raise the price of that product. The production of the import-competing good will thereby increase. An increase in production implies an increase in demand for factors of production. Consequently, the demand for and use of labour increases in the modern sector which leads to a reduction in the basic distortion.

In our model of labour surplus economies, we have not made any assumptions regarding the determination of the real wage rate in the modern or, as we have called them, formal sectors of the economy. In contrast to Negishi who assumed that the wage rate equals the average productivity of labour in the subsistence, or informal, part of the economy, we have made the assumption that the real wage is fixed and exogenously determined. However, as long as there is an excess supply of labour in the formal parts of the economy, which by definition is always the case in labour surplus economies, a basic distortion exists between the formal and the informal sectors of the economy.

Keeping this comment in mind, we now turn to the analysis of the relationship between social clauses and the distortions that may exist in full employment economies as well as in the formal parts of labour surplus economies.

Distortions and Social Clauses on Specific Working Conditions

In the previous sections of this chapter, we have analysed the economic effects of social clauses on various specific working conditions. The analysis has been made under an assumption of initial optimality with the exception of the basic distortion in labour surplus economies, which has been dealt with above. Under this assumption, it is obvious that the incorporation of social clauses on specific working conditions in the rules that govern international trade give rise to distortions as soon as they affect production in the economy or, in the case of labour surplus economies, have an effect on production in the formal parts of the economy.

A social clause on wages disturbs the allocation of resources, since it gives rise to a wage differential between manufacturing and non-manufacturing sectors of production. Although social clauses on hours of work and child labour will not affect the initial production mix in the formal parts of labour surplus economies, they clearly may do so in full employment economies. Regarding the clause on hours of work, it may, if efficiently supervised, give rise to a wage differential, whereas the clause on child labour may disturb the initial resource allocation by requiring a reallocation of child labour away from those production activities where they are most productive. Consequently, the production possibilities of the economies concerned are reduced. Finally, the social clause on occupational health and safety also gives rise to distortions. This is due to the fact that the social clause includes requirements relating to the working environment in the manufacturing industry. It is clear that such a limited regulation can be characterised as a sort of discriminatory taxation of this industry. Furthermore, the clause implies that producers in the manufacturing industry may not use the profit maximising technology. Hence, in comparison with the initial state, the production possibilities of the economy have been negatively affected by this clause.

With regard to the conclusion that social clauses on specific working conditions tend to give rise to distortions, it should be noted that the generalised theory of distortions, which has been worked out mainly by Bhagwati, presents clear-cut recommendations on domestic policy actions that can be taken in order to reduce or eliminate the distortions imposed by the social clauses.[40] For instance, if, after the introduction of a social clause on wages, labour is subsidised in manufacturing and an appropriate tax is levied on the use of labour in the extractive industry and agriculture, it would always be possible to re-establish the initial output mix. With regard to the clauses on hours of work, child labour and occupational health and safety, production tax-cum-subsidies can be used to reduce, but not eliminate, the distortions that may arise from such clauses.

Now, let us turn to the case where there is an initial distortion in the economy, or, in the case of labour surplus economies, in the formal part of the economy. On the basis of the generalised theory of distortions, social clauses on specific working conditions can be concluded to improve economic welfare only when working conditions in the export industry covered by the clauses are inferior to those in other parts of the economy. Empirically, this case can be characterised as a curiosity since, as a rule, in developing countries working conditions in the exporting manufacturing industry are far above those prevailing for instance in agriculture and mining. Nevertheless, if working conditions actually give rise to a distortion of the above type, social clauses on specific working conditions can be used to improve the welfare of the economy in question. However, for labour surplus economies, it is important to keep in mind that there is a risk that the basic distortion between the formal and the informal parts of the economy will be enlarged. The introduction of social clauses tends to lead to a decrease in manufacturing employment. Given that manufacturing is the labour-intensive industry, a reduction in manufacturing employment will lead to a lower level of employment in the formal part of the economy as a whole. As a result, the basic distortion between the formal and informal parts of the economy will increase.

Summary

In cases when social clauses on specific working conditions are directed against an economy that is in a Pareto optimal state, the clauses will give rise to a displacement of this optimum. However, we have noted that, for a social clause on wages, there is a possibility for domestic politicians to re-establish the initial output mix without running into conflict with the social clause.

In cases where social clauses on specific working conditions are directed against an economy that is initially in an inoptimal state, the incorporation of social clauses *may* give rise to welfare gains, provided that manufacturing is the sector in the economy that produces at a level above the Pareto optimal level. However, we should not forget that in labour surplus economies, the positive effects on the resource allocation in the formal parts of the economy, that may arise out of the introduction of social clauses, should be weighed against the enlarged distortion between the formal and informal parts of the economy that tends to accompany these clauses.

3.8 Concluding Remarks

This chapter has been devoted to an analysis of the economic effects of social clauses on various specific working conditions. In this section we will sum up the results of the analysis in order to state certain conclusions with regard to the relationships between, on the one hand, the different social clauses and, on the other hand, the employment, national income and income distribution in economies that have to change their working conditions, when social clauses are incorporated in the rules that govern international trade.

However, we will comment first on the simplifying assumption of perfect competition in the labour market that has underlied the analysis in this chapter. A discussion of the importance of this assumption for our results concerning social clauses on specific working conditions would seem to be highly warranted since, in Chapter 2, we criticised others for deriving results and making empirical conclusions on the basis of this assumption.

In Chapter 2, we found that the employment effect, and thereby also the production effect of unionisation, may be positive in the unionised sector when labour markets, in the absence of trade unions, could be characterised as monopsonistic markets. Similarly, if the producers in the sector covered by some of the social clauses on specific working conditions face an upward sloping supply curve of labour, it is possible that the clauses may give rise to positive production effects in this sector and negative effects in the rest of the economy. However, a necessary, but not sufficient, condition for these positive effects is that the marginal cost of employing labour becomes constant. In other words, all specific working conditions that affect the marginal costs of employing labour must be fixed by the social clauses at levels above the initial ones. If this condition is not fulfilled, the marginal cost of employing labour will be an increasing function and the monopsonist will face an upward shift in this cost function when the various cost-increasing social clauses are introduced. Consequently, in these cases, the results presented in this chapter in relation to the economic effects of social clauses will also be valid in the case of a monopsonistic labour market.

Given that the above condition is not satisfied, and from an empirical point of view this will not be too unrealistic an assumption, the assumption of perfect competition is not critical for the qualitative results that have been derived in this chapter.[41] Therefore, we continue by summing up our results without any further concern about the assumption of perfect competition in the labour market. Furthermore, we disregard the possibility of counteracting tax-cum-subsidies in the export economies concerned.

Social Clauses and Employment

Our analysis of social clauses on specific working conditions has been worked out within two analytical models, of which one has described an economy where full employment is always established while the other has been concerned with an economy which has a labour surplus at all relevant wage levels. By definition, it is only in the latter type of economy that social clauses can affect total employment or, more precisely, the employment in the formal parts of the economy.

With regard to the effects on the aggregate level of employment in the formal parts of labour surplus economies, we have found that the clauses on hours of work and child labour do not affect the total work effort, whereas the clauses on wages and occupational health and safety clearly have that effect. However, a social clause on hours of work may well increase the number of individuals that perform the work although it does not change the total number of hours worked. In the same way a clause on child labour may well give rise to increased adult employment and a reduction in the employment of child labour in the formal parts of the economy.

Due to the increased wages that must be paid in the manufacturing sector, a social clause on wages will have a negative effect on employment in the short run. If manufacturing is the labour-intensive industry, this negative effect will be enlarged in the longer run. Finally, the employment effects of a social clause on occupational health and safety are less clear-cut. Employment will increase in the short run when the clause requires changes to be made in the manufacturing working environment that lead to an increase in the marginal productivity of labour. In all other cases, the impact effect will be negative. In the longer run, all types of changes in the working environment, that take place as a consequence of the social clause, will give rise to negative employment effects, unless manufacturing is the capital-intensive industry.

Social Clauses and National Income

Closely related to the effects on employment are the effects on the national income. Social clauses that have an effect on the production in the economy also affect the national income. This holds for both full employment and for labour surplus economies. Furthermore, given the assumptions of perfectly competitive conditions, the absence of initial distortions in all factor and commodity markets, a given stock of capital and the assumption of internationally given commodity prices, we may conclude that the effect on the national income of an export economy, that has to change its working conditions when social clauses are incorporated in the rules that govern international trade, must be negative. This negative effect can be counteracted if either of these assumptions are replaced.

If the terms of trade of the economy or the stock of capital is positively affected by the introduction of social clauses, the negative effect on the national income will be counteracted. The terms of trade effect will be analysed in Chapter 4 where we compare the effects of a trade policy based on social clauses with a policy based on traditional trade policy measures. Regarding the effect on the stock of capital, this depends critically on the long run effect on the return to capital of the incorporation of social clauses in trade policy. In the preceding sections, we have found that this effect is clear-cut and negative in the case when social clauses are directed against an economy with a labour surplus. In the case of social clauses directed against exports from full employment economies, the effect on the return to capital is indeterminate.

Finally, if we depart from the assumption of no initial distortions in the economy, or in the formal parts of the economy in the case of labour surplus economies, the effects on the national income become even more complex. In these cases, there is a possibility that national income, like economic welfare, can be positively affected by the introduction of social clauses, assuming that production in manufacturing is above the Pareto optimal level prior to the introduction of the clause. In other cases, social clauses on specific working conditions will increase the initial distortion and reduce the national income.

Social Clauses and Income Distribution

The income distribution will also be affected by the introduction of social clauses that give rise to changes in working conditions in the country's export industry.

Starting with the effects on wage earners, we have found that, as a rule, the introduction of social clauses on specific working conditions that have an effect on production, also affect income distribution in favour of workers that are employed in the manufacturing export industry after the changes have taken place. It should be added that, although social clauses on child labour and hours of work do not affect production in the formal parts of labour surplus economies, they clearly may affect income distribution. The changes due to a clause on child labour may well be detrimental for large size families, since this clause will give rise to increased adult employment and a lower level of employment of child labour in the formal parts of the economy. Regarding the clause on hours of work, we have noted that in labour surplus economies, this clause tends to increase the number of workers in manufacturing as well as in the formal parts of the economy. Although this clause may lead to a reduction in working hours for each worker in manufacturing it can be expected to promote a more even income distribution in the economy.

In labour surplus economies, the return to land will be unaffected by the introduction of social clauses on specific working conditions. However, in full employment economies, the effects will be in the opposite direction in comparison with the effects on non-manufacturing wages. With respect to the return to capital, we have found that this will be negatively affected in labour surplus economies, whereas the effect, as a rule, is indeterminate in full employment economies. Finally, the incomes of mineowners have been found to be positively affected by the social clauses in labour surplus economies. As a rule, this will also be the case in full employment economies that face social clauses on specific working conditions.

Full Employment Versus Labour Surplus – A Final Comment

In this chapter, the analyses of social clauses on various specific working conditions have been worked out within two economic models that differ only in their basic labour market characteristics. One of the models is characterised by full employment while the other has a labour surplus at all relevant wage levels. We have found that the economic effects of the social clauses differ significantly between these two types of economies.

First, we have noted that clauses on hours of work and child labour will leave production unaffected when the covered economies are characterised by a labour surplus, whereas in the case of full employment economies, we have found that these clauses may well have an effect on production. Another difference is that in labour surplus economies, only the sector covered by the clauses will be affected in the short run, whereas in full employment economies other sectors of production will also be affected via the reallocation of labour that must occur in order to maintain full employment. Furthermore, in the case of labour surplus economies, agriculture, or in more general terms the sector which in addition to labour only uses sector specific factors of production is unaffected by the social clauses. However, in full employment economies the social clauses have a decided impact on this sector. We have also noted that factor intensities are critical for the direction of several of the adjustment effects in full employment economies, while, as a rule, they do not matter for the qualitative effects in labour surplus economies. An important example of this difference is given by the total long run effect on the return to capital. The impact of social clauses on production in labour surplus economies always exerts a negative effect on the return to capital, whereas in principle the effect is indeterminate in full employment economies. In fact, provided that manufacturing is the labour-intensive industry social clauses on hours of work and occupational health and safety may produce a positive effect.[42]

It is obvious, from the differences noted above, that a traditional approach, with full employment as the basic labour market characteristic, may be inappropriate in the case of less developed economies with surplus labour. In fact, the traditional analysis may lead to conclusions that are contrary to those obtained from an analysis where surplus labour is explicitly included.

Appendix: The Derivation of the Mathematical Expressions in Chapter 3

In this appendix we will present some intermediary steps of the derivation of the mathematical expressions presented in Chapter 3. As with the analyses in this chapter, the presentation will be divided into two parts dealing respectively with the full employment economy and the labour surplus economy.

The Full Employment Economy

A Social Clause on Wages. By using Cramer's rule we can solve equations (13)–(16), (18) and (26) for each of the two exogenous variables, dw_M and dK_M respectively, keeping the other one constant.

For short run changes in the manufacturing wage level, w_M, we can then obtain the expressions in Table 3.3.

As concerns the effects of the reallocation of capital, the same procedure yields:

$$dL_M/dK_M = -M_{KL}/M_{LL},$$

$$dL_E/dK_M = -(1/D)(p_E M_{LL} E_{KL} + M_{KL} A_{LL}),$$

$$dL_A/dK_M = (1/D) p_E (M_{LL} E_{KL} - M_{KL} E_{LL}),$$

$$dw/dK_M = A_{LL}(dL_A/dK_M),$$

$$dv/dK_M = A_{RL}(dL_A/dK_M),$$

$$dr_M/dK_M = p_M (M_{LL} M_{KK} - M^2_{LK})/M_{LL},$$

and

$$dr_E/dK_M = (1/D) p_E [(M_{LL} E_{KK} - M_{KL} E_{KL}) A_{LL} + p_E M_{LL}(E_{LL} E_{KK} - E^2_{LK})],$$

where

$$D = -M_{LL}(p_E E_{LL} + A_{LL}) < 0$$

By making use of Euler's theorem it can be proved that

$$E_{LL} = [(\theta_E - 1) E_L/L_E] - (K_E/L_E) E_{LK},$$

$$E_{KK} = [(\theta_E - 1) E_K/K_E] - (L_E/K_E) E_{KL} ,$$

and accordingly for M_{LL} and M_{KK} respectively, where θ_i represents the degree of homogeneity of the production function in sector i, i = E, M.

By using these expressions, keeping in mind that manufacturing has been assumed to display constant returns to scale, i.e. $\theta_M = 1$, whereas the extractive industry has been assumed to display decreasing returns to scale in the use of labour and capital, i.e. $\theta_E < 1$, we can expand the expressions above so that they take the form presented in Table 3.4.

Social Clauses on Hours of Work, Child Labour and Occupational Health and Safety. By the same procedure as the one followed above, the mathematical expressions for short run and longer run adustment effects of social clauses on hours of work, child labour and occupational health and safety can be derived.

With the exception of dr_M/dt_M in Table 3.15, all the mathematical expressions in Tables 3.8, 3.12 and 3.15 can be derived directly by applying Cramer's rule to the system of equations (12)–(16) and (18). As concerns the expression mentioned above, Cramer's rule yields:

$$dr_M/dt_M = (p_M/D)[p_M(p_E E_{LL} + A_{LL}) \times (M_{LK}M_{tL} - M_{LL}M_{tK}) - p_E E_{LL} A_{LL} M_{tK}]$$

By making use of Euler's theorem, this expression can be expanded to the corresponding expression in Table 3.15.

Turning to the longer run adjustment effects of social clauses on hours of work, child labour and occupational health and safety, we solve equations (12)–(16) and (18) for exogenous changes in the manufacturing use of capital. By making use of Cramer's rule on this system of equations we obtain directly the expressions for dL_M/dK_M and dL_E/dK_M that are presented in Table 3.9. Furthermore, we obtain:

$$dL_A/dK_M = (1/D) p_M p_E (M_{LL}E_{KL} - M_{KL}E_{LL}) ,$$

$$dr_M/dK_M = (1/D) p_M[p_E A_{LL}\alpha(M_{LK}E_{LK} - M_{KK}E_{LL}) - p_M(p_E E_{LL} + A_{LL})(M_{LL}M_{KK} - M^2_{LK})]$$

and

$$dr_E/dK_M = (1/D)p_E[p_M A_{LL}(M_{LL}E_{KK} - M_{KL}E_{KL}) + p_E(p_M M_{LL} + \alpha A_{LL})(E_{LL}E_{KK} - E^2_{LK})]$$

By applying Euler's theorem to these expressions we can derive the expressions presented in Table 3.9.

Finally, we can solve equations (12)–(18) for the total long run effect on the marginal return to capital of a wage differential, α, a change in the total labour force, L, and a technical change in the manufacturing industry, t_M, respectively, which yields:

$$dr/d\alpha = (1/D)wp_M p_E[p_E(E_{LL}E_{KK} - E^2_{LK})M_{LK} + A_{LL}(M_{LK}E_{KK} - M_{KK}E_{KL})],$$

$$dr/dL = (1/D)p_M p_E[p_M E_{KL}A_{LL}(M_{LL}M_{KK} - M^2_{LK}) + p_E M_{KL}A_{LL}(E_{LL}E_{KK} - E^2_{LK})]$$

and

$$dr/dt_M = (1/D)p_M p_E\{p_E(E_{LL}E_{KK} - E^2_{LK}) \times [A_{LL}M_{Kt} + p_M(M_{LL}M_{Kt} - M_{LK}M_{Lt})] + p_M A_{LL}[E_{KL}(M_{KK}M_{Lt} - M_{LK}M_{Kt}) + E_{KK}(M_{LL}M_{Kt} - M_{LK}M_{Lt})]\},$$

where

$$D = p^2_E(E_{LL}E_{KK} - E^2_{LK})(p_M M_{LL} + A_{LL}) + p^2_M(M_{LL}M_{KK} - M^2_{LK})(p_E E_{LL} + A_{LL}) + p_M p_E A_{LL}(M_{LL}E_{KK} + M_{KK}E_{LL} - 2M_{LK}E_{LK})$$

These expressions can be expanded by means of Euler's theorem so that expressions (27)–(29) are obtained.

The Labour Surplus Economy

By the same procedure as the one used for deriving the mathematical expressions for the effects of social clauses in a full employment economy, we can derive the expressions for the effects in a labour surplus economy.

By using Cramer's rule we can solve the system of equations (19)–(23) and (25) for exogenous changes in the manufacturing wage, w_M, the technology used in the manufacturing sector, t_M, and the manufacturing use of capital, K_M.

As concerns the expressions for the short run effects of exogenous changes in w_M and t_M, that are presented in Tables 3.5 and 3.16, only the expression for dr_M/dt_M in Table 3.16 requires additional comments. The use of Cramer's rule on the above system of equations yields:

$$dr_M/dt_M = -(p_M/M_{LL})(M_{LK}M_{tL} - M_{LL}M_{tK})$$

Making use of Euler's theorem and the assumption of a linearly homogeneous manufacturing production function, we can expand the above expression and obtain the one presented in Table 3.16.

Turning to the longer run adjustment effects, only two expressions require some comments, in the sense that they do not follow directly from the use of Cramer's rule on the equations above. First, as concerns manufacturing employment the direct solution yields:

$$dL_M/d\bar{K}_M = -M_{KL}/M_{LL}$$

which can be rewritten by means of Euler's theorem as the expression presented in Table 3.6. Secondly, the use of Cramer's rule yields:

$$dr_M/dK_M = (p_M/M_{LL})(M_{LL}M_{KK} - M^2_{LK}).$$

Since the manufacturing industry has been assumed to display constant returns to scale, the use of Euler's theorem yields $dr_M/dK_M = 0$.

Notes

1. See e.g. EEC (1980), Department of Labour, Canada (1979), US Department of Labor (1978) and ICFTU (1979).
2. For an analysis of a social clause on labour market discrimination, see Hansson and Lundahl (1981a).
3. Graham (1948), p. 284.
4. For a discussion, see Jones (1977).
5. Gruen and Corden (1970).
6. See also Lewis (1954), and his analysis of economic development in an economy with an 'unlimited' supply of labour.
7. Cf. Lewis (1954).

8. Batra and Seth (1977).

9. For comments on the labour market assumptions, see section 3.8. For the relationship between micro- and macro-production functions, see Bentzel and Johansson (1959).

10. For an extensive description and analysis of the different possible outcomes in the case of factor price differentials, see e.g. the works by Jones (1971) and Magee (1973).

11. Mayer (1974).

12. Note that we assume $\alpha = 1$ in the initial long run equilibrium.

13. For the derivation of the mathematical expressions that will be presented in the sections below, see the Appendix.

14. See note 13.

15. For instance, see Säve-Söderbergh (1978a, b) and US Department of Labor (1978).

16. Blum (1925), p. 64.

17. Information received from the ILO.

18. For a more general discussion and analysis of the aims and efficiency of minimum-wage legislation, see e.g. Smith (1967), Franklin (1969), Lester (1969), Ch. 16, ILO (1968), Watanabe (1976) and Starr (1981). For theoretical analyses of minimum wages within a general equilibrium framework, see e.g. Johnson (1969) and Brecher (1974). Johnson's analysis concerns a closed economy whereas Brecher's article exclusively deals with a general minimum wage.

19. See Chapter 1.

20. The Convention on Hours of Work adopted in 1919 has, up to July 1981, been ratified by 44 countries. The Forty-Hour Week Convention from 1935 has, up to July 1981, been ratified by seven countries.

21. For an explanation of the increasing incomes of mineowners, see the summary in section 3.3.

22. Mendelievich (1979), which is the main source of this section.

23. The small proportion can partly be explained by the fact that very small children are also included in the total amount of children whereas for biological reasons they cannot be expected to take part in work.

24. The studies on child labour in Greece, India and Peru are included in Mendelievich (1979). Child labour in Hong Kong is analysed in Porter (1975). For analyses of the reasons for and effects of child labour, see also Hamilton (1975).

25. Rybczynski (1955).

26. See Hansson and Lundahl (1981b) and references therein.

27. Note that $\alpha = 1$ in this case.

28. By solving equations (12)–(18) for the long run effects of a change in the labour force we obtain:

$$dw/dL = (1/D)p_M p_E A_{LL} M_{LL}(E_{LL}E_{KK} - E^2_{LK}) < 0$$

where D is identical to D in (27), $D < 0$.

29. This expression has been derived by solving equations (12)–(18) for the long run effects of a change in the labour force.

30. See note 21.

31. See e.g. US Department of Labor (1978).

32. See e.g. Säve-Söderbergh (1978a, b), LO and TCO (1978).

33. See ILO (1980); see also section 1.1 of the present study.

34. Hicks (1932). Strictly speaking, Hicks uses the terms capital-saving and labour-saving, whereas in our analysis of negative technical changes we prefer to

use the terms labour-using and capital-using, respectively. See also Blaug (1963) and Södersten (1964), Ch. 3. Södersten contains an extensive analysis of technical changes within a two-sector general equilibrium model.

35. Note that $\alpha = 1$ in this case.

36. For an explanation of the change in the income for mineowners, see the summary of section 3.3.

In the case when not only wages, but also other working conditions such as occupational health and safety, are included in the utility functions of the workers, a social clause on occupational health and safety can be expected to give rise to a wage differential, $\alpha = w_M/w < 1$. However, we ignore this potential effect of the social clause in question since wages can be expected to have a predominant weight in the utility functions compared to other working conditions in those economies that can be subjected to the social clause.

37. The effect will be negative if $M_{Kt} \leqq 0$ and $K_M/L_M \geqq K_E/L_E$.

38. Nath (1969), p. 19.

39. Negishi (1972), p. 170.

40. For instance, see Bhagwati (1971) and Bhagwati *et al.* (1969).

41. Only in the case when the supply of labour is a function of wages and does not depend on other working conditions, can the introduction of a social clause on wages satisfy the above condition. Clauses on other specific working conditions cannot be expected to satisfy the condition since the wage always will be important for the supply of labour.

42. A positive long run effect on the return to capital can also arise in the case of a social clause on wages, namely if the clause gives rise to a complete industrial specialisation.

4 SOCIAL CLAUSES AND ALTERNATIVE TRADE POLICY MEASURES – A COMPARATIVE ANALYSIS

4.1 Introduction

Demands for social clauses that have been advanced in the trade policy debate have been frequently met by arguments based on a fear of increased protectionism. This is a natural reaction if one considers the introduction of social clauses as a means of adding new trade restrictions to those already at work today. However, the advancement of new trade policy measures, in this case social clauses, in trade negotiations, can equally well be viewed as substitutes for some of the old policy measures, i.e. as reforming rather than increasing protectionism.

When we analysed different forms of social clauses in a free trade world in Chapters 2 and 3, this substitution aspect was excluded by definition. In this chapter, we will complete the analysis by comparing the different forms of social clauses with other policies that can be used to restrict international trade. The aim is to analyse the equivalences and non-equivalences of cost-increasing social clauses on the one hand and tariffs, import quotas and voluntary export restraints on the other. This analysis ought to enable us to clarify the relative merits of different types of trade policy measures. The purpose of the analysis is also to clarify whether the introduction of social clauses in the rules that govern international trade provides an efficient means for the improvement of working conditions in the export industries of countries that are at present below the standard required by the social clauses. It should be remembered that social clauses force the economies towards a choice between changes in the working conditions and the risk of being confronted with other trade barriers in their export markets, due to substandard working conditions.

Studies of equivalences and non-equivalences between different trade barriers have been worked out by many economists.[1] Most of the analyses have been partial equilibrium analyses of the price and quantity effects of the imposition of different trade barriers on the importing economy. In conformity with the previous studies, our analysis will be of a partial equilibrium nature concerned with the static equivalences and non-equivalences of different trade barriers from the point of view of the importing economy.

The use of partial analysis in this chapter is also motivated by our desire to find quantitative as well as qualitative non-equivalences with respect to prices and quantities between the use of different trade barriers. A general equilibrium analysis of the kind we have used in Chapter 3 is insufficient for this purpose, whereas a traditional partial analysis clearly provides such information. In section 4.3 the results derived from the partial analysis will be used as inputs in the analysis of the effects of the different policy measures on a discriminated export economy. Similar to the analysis in Chapter 3, this latter analysis deals with the effects on national income, employment and income distribution.

The Meaning of Equivalence

An analysis of equivalences and non-equivalences of different policy measures must start out from one given equivalence that can be used as a point of reference. For instance, Bhagwati analyses the equivalences between tariffs and import quotas that are set in such a manner that they will give rise to the same quantity of imports.[2] Other starting points, that have been used by McCulloch in her analysis of the relative welfare cost of tariffs and import quotas under different assumptions regarding the motives for protection, are output equivalence, price equivalence and profit equivalence.[3] In these cases the different policy measures are determined so that they give rise to the same domestic output, the same domestic price and the same monopoly profit for the domestic producer, respectively.

In this chapter, we will analyse import equivalent policy measures. In the literature, import equivalence refers to the aggregated imports of a specific country. Furthermore, as a rule, the measures are assumed to cover imports from all foreign supply sources, to be non-discriminatory. However, since the main interest of the present study is concerned with the effects on export economies that do not comply with the minimum labour standards that are assumed to be incorporated in the various social clauses, we will compare the effects of different discriminatory policy measures. In other words, we will analyse the effects of tariffs, import quotas and voluntary export restraints that are designed in such a way that they only cover imports from the countries that do not comply with the requirements stated in the social clauses. In the rest of this chapter, *import equivalent policy measures* are defined as policy measures that give rise to the same import level from a specific economy or group of economies.

Country Assumptions

An analysis of the effects of different trade policy measures requires assumptions relating to the 'size' of the economies involved in trade. If the economy that imposes the policy is small enough in the international market for the commodity concerned, its activities including its policy actions will have no influence on the international market situation. The size of the individual economies involved in trade will consequently play a central role in the formation of trade policy in different economies. In this chapter we assume that the economy, or group of economies, imposing the different policy measures is sufficiently large to affect the international market for the commodity in question. With regard to the *individual* export economies, towards which the policy measures are directed, we retain the small country assumption employed in Chapter 3. However, taken together as a group, these economies are assumed to be of sufficient size so that changes in their aggregate supply affect the international price.

Policy Measures

Before we proceed with the analysis, we will comment on the policy measures that we are going to compare in this chapter.

Social clauses have already been presented and are consequently assumed to be well known to the reader. In the choice between facing traditional trade barriers and changing working conditions in order to meet the requirements of the social clauses, it is initially assumed that the export economies concerned choose to alter their working conditions. It is also assumed that these changes are cost-increasing since they are not made in the absence of external pressure. Although different cost-increasing or protective social clauses affect production in the export industries in different ways, it is assumed that they give rise to a constant or increasing additional cost per unit produced. Furthermore, we assume that these changes are reflected in a reduced supply of the commodity in question from the economies covered by the clauses. In the diagrammatic analysis we assume this shift to be parallel. When this assumption is critical for the results derived, it will be stated explicitly.

With respect to *tariffs* and *import quotas*, these are well known and do not need any further comments. However, the fourth type of trade barriers included in our analysis, *voluntary export restraints*, may require some comment before we introduce them into the analysis.

Voluntary export restraints, hereafter called VERs, can be defined as export limitations administered by one or more of the exporting countries. As a rule, the enforcement of VERs is a result of negotiations with the importing economies. The exporters are more or less forced to impose VERs to avoid, or reduce, the risks for market disruptions due to other protectionistic measures that can be imposed by the importers. Bergsten has given a detailed definition that makes clear that the VERs can take many various forms:

> VERs are limitations on export sales (a) administered by one or more exporting countries or industries (b) on the volume or value of their sales (c) to a single foreign market or several markets, or (rarely) the world as a whole (d) triggered by pressure from the government or industry of the importing country or countries (e) carried out either bilaterally or within a multilateral framework (f) sometimes explicitly authorized or guided by domestic law, and sometimes not.[4]

In our analysis we will define VERs in volume terms. The most well known example of VERs is the Multifiber Agreement that governs large parts of the international trade in textile and clothing commodities. Other examples are those used in the United States to protect steel and meat producers. Recently, the international trade in automobiles has also been restricted by VERs.

4.2 Comparative Trade Policy Analysis – The Importing Economy

In this section we will analyse the equivalences and non-equivalences between different discriminatory and import equivalent trade policy measures from the point of view of the importing or the 'protectionist' economy. In the analysis, the diagrams used describe both the foreign supply confronting the importing economy and the domestic market situation in this economy.[5]

Figure 4.1

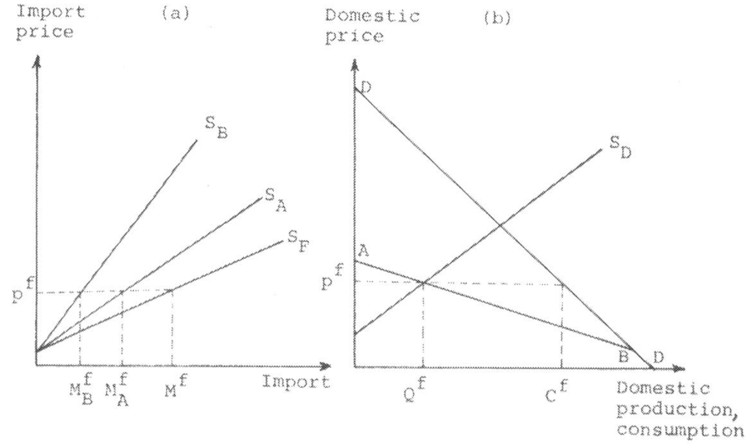

In Figure 4.1, it should be noted that the foreign supply curve, S_F, is a net supply curve, i.e. it describes the foreign supply net of foreign demand. In Figure 4.1(a), the foreign supply curve is divided into two curves, S_A describing the supply from economies that are required to change their working conditions in the export industry following the introduction of the social clauses, and S_B describing the supply from other foreign sources. The reason for this division is that we will analyse discriminatory trade policy means, i.e. measures that only cover imports from some specific foreign sources.

In Figure 4.1(b), DD represents the importing economy's domestic demand for the commodity and S_D represents the supply from domestic producers. Assuming free trade, the domestic producers meet a residual demand curve ABD. This curve has been derived by subtracting the foreign supply from the total domestic demand. In a world characterised by free trade with perfect competition in domestic production as well as in importing and foreign exporting, the domestic consumption will be C^f units, domestic production will be Q^f units and the import will be equal to $C^f - Q^f = M^f$ units. The domestic price and the international price will coincide and be equal to p^f.

In the following analysis, we will compare the effects on prices and quantities of different import equivalent policy measures, i.e. measures that give rise to the same quantity of imports from a specific foreign source, denoted as A. The analysis will be made under various assumptions with regard to the competitiveness in domestic production, importing and foreign exporting, respectively. For pedagogical reasons, we start with the case of perfect competition in all these activities.

Perfect Competition in Domestic Production, Importing and Foreign Exporting

The analysis starts from the situation described by Figure 4.1, where M^f units are imported at the price p^f. Following the introduction of a social clause, we compare the effects of this policy with the effects of other trade barriers that give rise to the same import quantity from the specific country or group of countries that are required to change their working conditions in order to meet the requirements of the clause.

As was described above, the introduction of protective social clauses will reduce the supply from countries covered by the clause. From an importing country's point of view, the effects of protective social clauses express themselves in terms of a reduced foreign supply of the commodity. In Figure 4.2(a) this is illustrated by the shift in the foreign supply curve S_A to $S^s{}_A$. A shift in S_A will lead to a shift in the total foreign supply curve S_F to $KIS^s{}_F$.

As a result of the shifts in foreign supply, the domestic producers will meet a new residual demand curve, A'B'BD. In the importing economy the market is cleared at the price $p^s{}_D$, with a domestic supply equal to Q^s, and a domestic consumption equal to C^s. Consequently, imports are equal to $C^s - Q^s = M^s$. We note that the introduction of the clause increases the price paid for imports. As there have been no changes in the costs of production in foreign sources not covered by the social clauses there will be an increase in imports from these sources, B, whereas imports from export economies, subject to protective social clauses, A, will decrease.

As an alternative policy we now introduce a discriminatory tariff that is set at a level that gives rise to the same quantity of

Figure 4.2: Effects of Discriminatory Policy Measures that are Import Equivalent With Regard to Imports from A – the Case of Perfect Competition in Domestic Production, Exporting and Importing

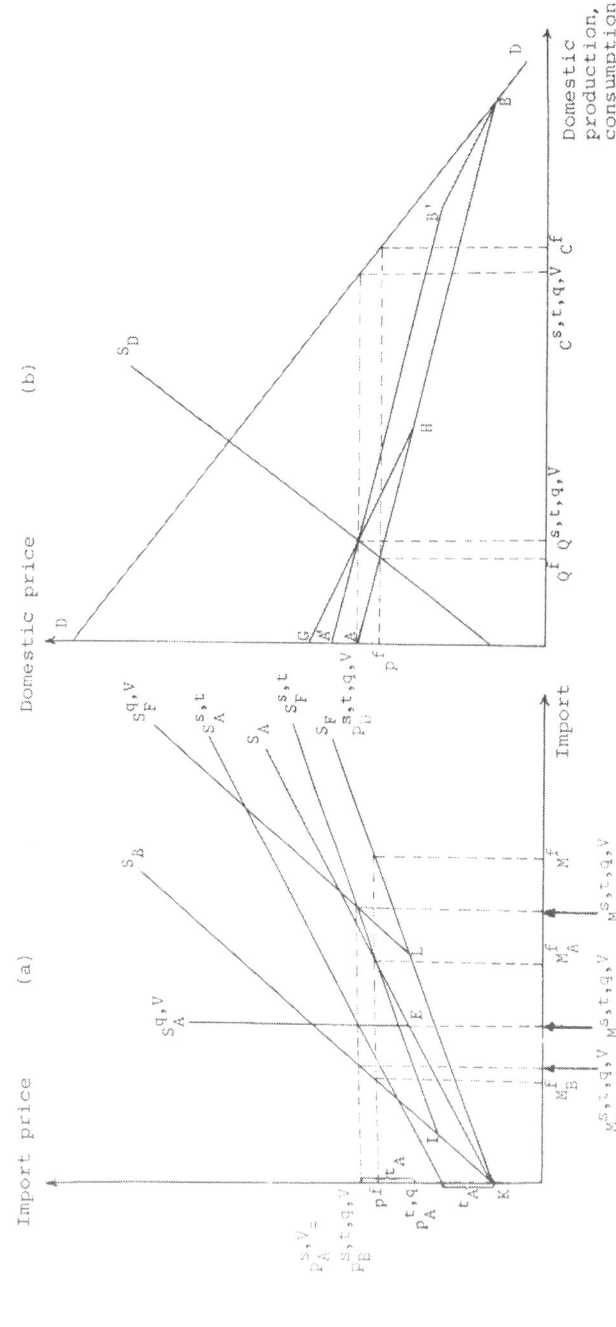

Note: s = social clause, t = tariff, q = import quota, V = voluntary export restraint (VER).

imports from A as in the case of the social clause. If the tariff is equal to t_A per unit imported from A, the supply curve S_A shifts to $S^t{}_A$. Consequently, the aggregate supply curve S_F also shifts upwards to $KIS^t{}_F$. If the tariff should be import equivalent to protective social clauses, i.e. $M^s{}_A = M^t{}_A$ the shifts in the foreign supply curves must be such that given perfect market conditions, the effects on domestic price, consumption and import must be equal. However, there is one difference between the use of social clauses and discriminatory tariffs, namely, the price paid for imports. It has been observed that in the case of social clauses, a reduced foreign supply may be explained by increased costs of production in the export economies subject to the social clauses. Consequently, in this case, the price paid for imports will be the same regardless of the foreign source. If we turn to import prices under a discriminatory tariff regime, we note that there will be one price for imports from the discriminated economy or group of economies, A, and one price for imports from other foreign sources, B. Under a discriminatory tariff regime a tariff must be paid for imports from A but not for imports from B. Finally, we note that the price paid for imports from non-covered foreign sources, B, will be equal to the price paid for imports under a social clause regime, whereas the price paid for imports from the discriminated economy will be forced down to a level below the free trade level, to $p^t{}_A$ in Figure 4.2(a). In other words, the tariff will be divided between domestic consumers in the importing economy and the discriminated foreign producers.

An alternative way of obtaining the same level of imports from A is to use an appropriate import quota that is discriminatorily directed against A. A policy of this type would make the foreign supply curve S_A completely inelastic above point E in Figure 4.2(a). This change would affect the total foreign supply that is directed against the importing economy. In Figure 4.2(a) this is illustrated by the change of the curve S_F to $KLS^q{}_F$. In the domestic market, the changes in the foreign supply curves would be reflected in a change in the residual domestic demand curve, which moves to GHBD. Given the assumption of perfect competitive market conditions, we conclude that this policy will produce the same effects as the tariff, except in relation to the distribution of the rents that arise out of importing from A. Under a tariff regime, imports from A yield tariff revenues, whereas under an import equivalent import quota regime, the same amount will go to the import quota holders or, if the quotas are auctioned in a competitive market, to the government in the importing economy.

Finally, the importing economy can force the export economy A to restrain its exports, by imposing a VER such that the exports from A to the actual importing economy equal $M^s{}_A$. This type of policy will affect the market in exactly the same way as discriminatory and import equivalent import quotas with the exception of the rent associated with imports from A. In the case of a VER and perfect competition in the import activities this rent will be competed away from the importers. Consequently, the price paid for imports from A will equal the price paid for this import under an import equivalent social clause regime.

Monopoly in Domestic Production, Perfect Competition in Importing and Foreign Exporting

If we depart from the assumption of perfect competition in domestic production and assume that this production is carried out by a monopolist, we find the situation described in Figure 4.3. Assuming that the domestic monopolist is a profit maximiser, we know that the equilibrium for the monopolist is found where the marginal revenue, MR, equals the marginal cost of production, MC. Free trade and perfect competition in importing and exporting will give a domestic price equal to p^f, with a domestic production equal to Q^f and a domestic consumption equal to C^f. Consequently $M^f = C^f - Q^f$ units will be imported at the international price p^f.

In the same way as in the case of perfect competition in domestic production, importing and foreign exporting, we can now introduce different trade policy measures that give rise to the same level of protection with regard to imports from A. We start by introducing a social clause. In the same way as in the previously analysed case, the social clause is assumed to increase the costs of production in A. Consequently, the shifts in the supply curves S_A and S_F and the demand curve facing the domestic producer are similar to the previous case. The new domestic price will equal $p^s{}_D$. At this price C^s units will be domestically consumed of which Q^s units will come from the domestic producer and the remaining M^s units will be imported. Imports will be distributed between $\bar{M}_A$ units from A and $M^s{}_B$ units from B. By the same line of reasoning as in the previous case, the price paid for imports from the two sources will be equal to the domestic price.

Figure 4.3: Effects of Discriminatory Policy Measures that are Import Equivalent With Regard to Imports from A – the Case of Monopoly in Domestic Production

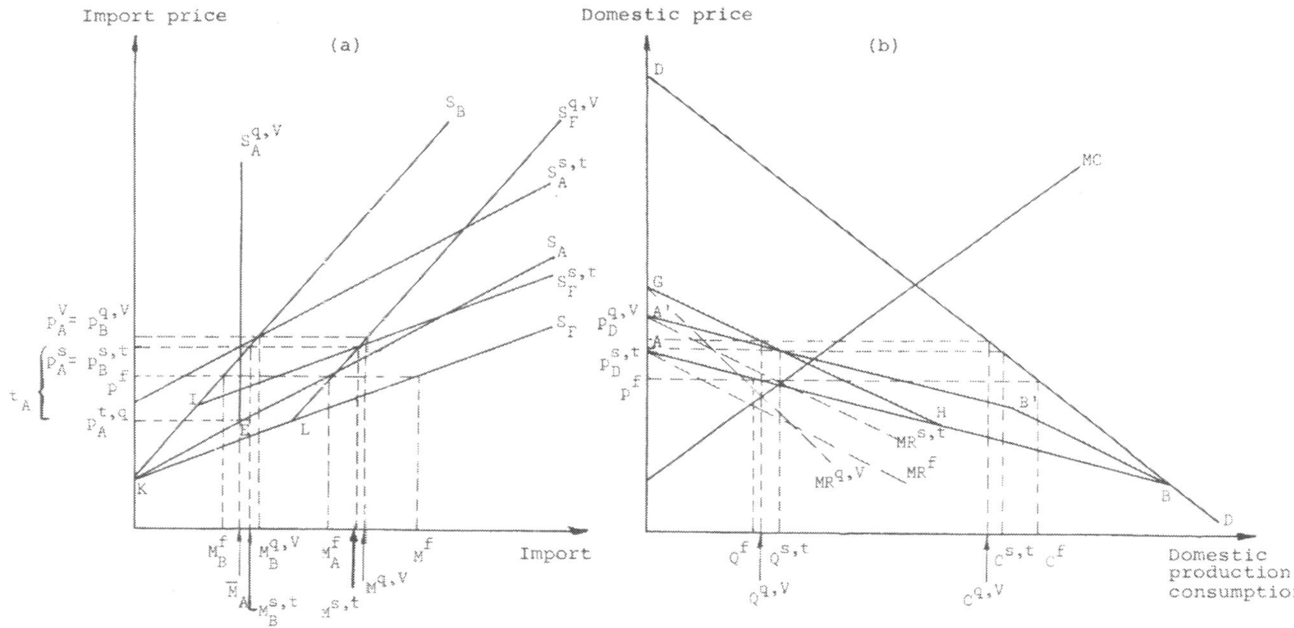

As the method and notation in Figure 4.3 are identical to the method and notation used in Figure 4.2 for the introduction of the other trade policy measures, it is not necessary to repeat the steps of analysis. With reference to Figure 4.3, it may be concluded that most of the equivalences that existed in relation to perfect competition do not apply to the case of monopoly in domestic production. The equivalences that still exist are those between import equivalent import quotas and VERs with respect to the effects on domestic price, production and consumption and, consequently, on the level of imports. Furthermore, we note that the domestic price increase is greater in the case of import quotas and VERs than is the case when import equivalent tariffs or social clauses are used. This can be explained by the fact that in the case of a social clause or a tariff, the domestic monopolist knows that when the domestic price is raised, import competition will increase both from discriminated and non-discriminated foreign sources, whereas in the case of an import quota or a VER the increased import competition can only come from non-discriminated countries. We also note that the price paid for imports from the discriminated economy or economies, A, will be the same for tariffs and import quotas, whereas VERs and social clauses give rise to a higher price for this import. Finally, it should be noted that the equivalences between social clauses and tariffs, as illustrated in Figure 4.3, depend critically on the assumed parallel shifts in the foreign supply curves when social clauses and tariffs are introduced. If social clauses give rise to an increasing additional cost per unit produced in the discriminated economy or group of economies, the equivalences indicated in Figure 4.3 will no longer be valid. In this case, the effect of social clauses on prices and quantities will lie between those of tariffs on the one hand, and import quotas and VERs on the other.

Monopoly in Exporting in A, Perfect Competition in Exporting in B, Domestic Production and Importing

Up to now we have assumed that international trade is characterised by perfect competition. Let us now remove the assumption of perfect competition for exports from A, whilst retaining the assumption of perfect competition for both exporting in B and importing. Furthermore, we reintroduce the assumption of perfect competition for domestic production.

Figure 4.4: Effects of Discriminatory Policy Measures that are Import Equivalent With Regard to Imports from A – the Case of Export Monopoly in A

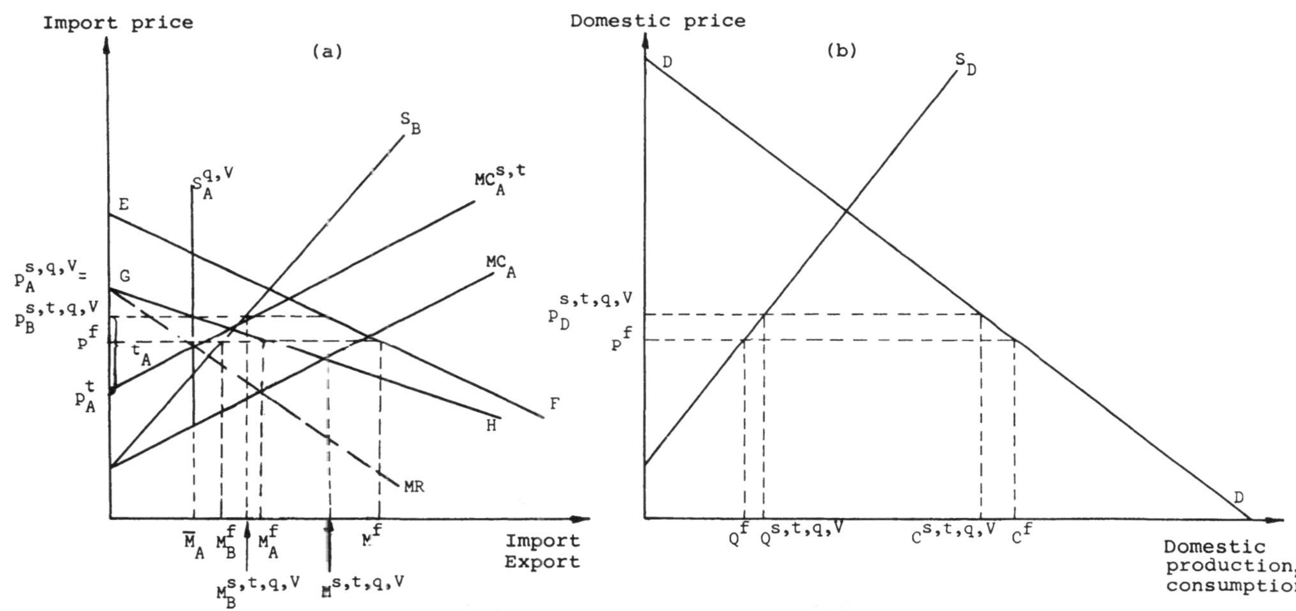

Figure 4.4(b) describes the situation in the importing economy. The total demand for the commodity concerned is represented by the curve denoted DD, and the domestic supply is described by the curve denoted S_D. By subtracting the domestic supply from total demand, we obtain the curve EF in Figure 4.4(a). This curve denotes the demand for imports. By subtracting the supply from B from this import demand curve we derive the relevant demand curve GH for the monopolist in A. From this demand curve, the monopolistic exporter in A deduces the marginal revenue curve associated with exporting, MR. Finally, the monopolist's marginal cost connected with exporting to the protective economy is represented by the curve MC_A.

If we assume that the export monopolist in A maximises the profits from exporting, the free trade equilibrium is given by the intersection between the MR and MC curves. The quantity M^f_A is exported from A. At the resulting price p^f, M^f_B units are exported from non-discriminated foreign sources, B. By introducing the different trade policy measures considered, we find that import equivalent social clauses, import quotas and VERs are also equivalent with respect to domestic and import prices. This equivalence also holds with respect to domestic consumption, production and imports, both in aggregate terms and in relation to each of the trading partners. If an import equivalent tariff against imports from A is introduced as an alternative to one of these trade barriers, all but one of the equivalences mentioned above will persist. The non-equivalence between tariffs and the other import equivalent policies is found in the price paid for imports from the discriminated foreign source, A. The underlying reason for this non-equivalence is that a tariff must be paid for imports from A under a tariff regime. Consequently, a tariff regime will give rise to a lower price paid for imports from A than the price paid under alternative trade policy regimes.

Monopoly in Exporting in B, Perfect Competition in Exporting in A, Domestic Production and Importing

We shall now examine the case where perfect competition exists in the export sector of the discriminated economy, A, while monopoly conditions prevail in export economies that are not covered by the discriminatory policy. Following the same line of analysis as presented in the section above, we find that the imposition of different trade policy measures, in order to restrict

Figure 4.5: Effects of Discriminatory Policy Measures that are Import Equivalent With Regard to Imports from A – the Case of Export Monopoly in B

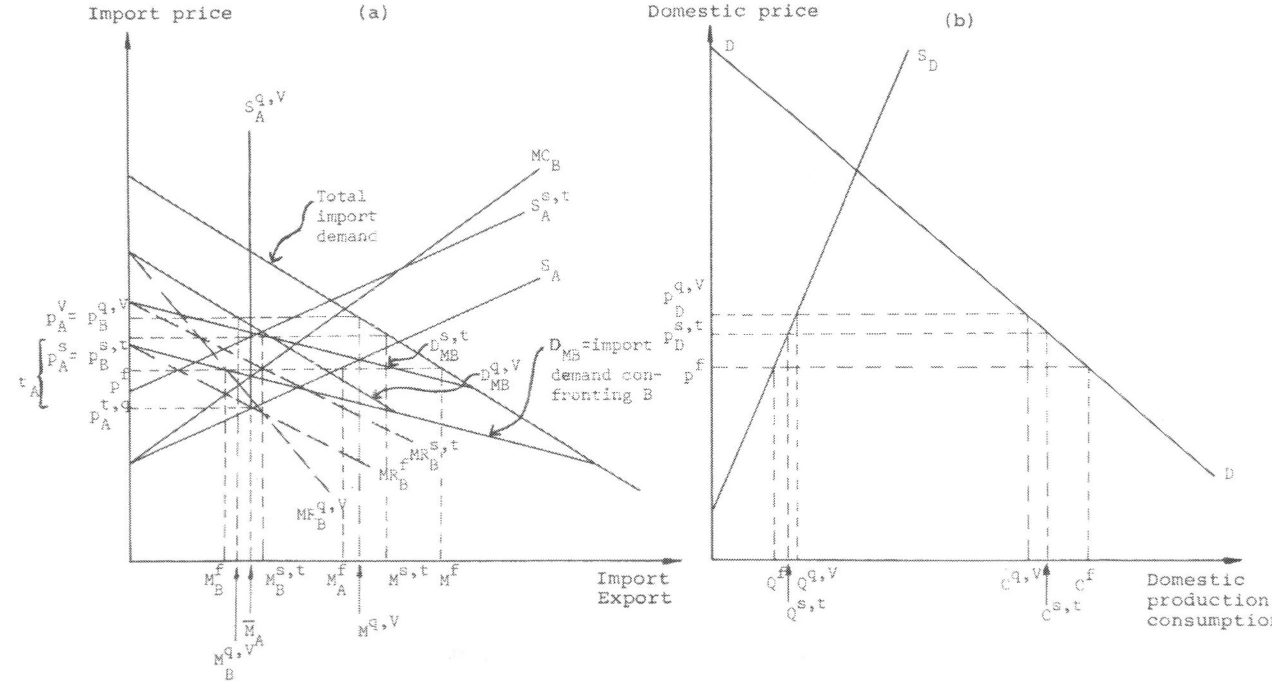

imports from the discriminated economy, A, to a given amount $\bar{M}_A$, will give rise to the price and quantity effects that are described in Figure 4.5.

As in the case of monopoly in domestic production, the equivalences between tariffs and social clauses, as indicated by the figure, depend critically on the manner in which the supply curve of the discriminated economy is assumed to shift. The relevant equivalences in this case are between import quotas and VERs with respect to quantities and the price paid for imports from the export monopoly in the non-discriminated economies, and the equivalence between tariffs and import quotas with respect to the price paid for imports from the discriminated economy.

Moreover, in the case of a social clause or a tariff, the export monopolist in the non-discriminated economies, B, knows that when the export price, p_B, is raised, competition will increase both from discriminated exporters and domestic producers in the importing economy, whereas in the case of an import quota or a VER only the latter group can increase their supply in the market concerned. Consequently, the price of exports from the export monopolist, and thereby the domestic price in the importing economy, will be highest for VERs and import quotas.

Monopoly in Importing, Perfect Competition in Domestic Production and Foreign Exporting

Finally, we now will analyse the case when there is an import monopoly. Domestic production as well as foreign exporting are assumed to be characterised by perfect competition. This case is illustrated in Figure 4.6.

As the monopolist is the single importer of the commodity concerned, he faces a marginal cost curve connected with importing, MCI, and a corresponding marginal revenue curve, MRI. The importer maximises profits at the import level where these two curves intercept.

Under free trade the profit maximising import quantity equals M^f units. These units are imported at the price p^f_M and sold in the domestic market at the price p^f_D. At this price, a total of C^f units will be consumed in the importing economy and Q^f units will be domestically produced.

The analysis of introducing different trade policy measures can be conducted in the same way as in the previous sections. The resulting equivalences and non-equivalences are described in

Figure 4.6. We conclude that when there is an import monopoly, import quotas and VERs will be equivalent in all respects considered. Furthermore, we note that social clauses will be non-equivalent to tariffs, import quotas and VERs. The equivalences between social clauses and tariffs as indicated in Figure 4.6 depend critically on the assumed form of the shift of the foreign supply curves. In particular, we note the non-equivalence between social clauses and the other policy measures considered in relation to the price paid for imports from A. As there is only one importer, the import price will be competed down to the level of the marginal costs of production on which the foreign supply is based. The price paid for imports from A will differ between the two groups of trade policy measures since tariffs, import quotas and VERs do not affect the costs of production in A, whereas social clauses have been assumed to have this effect.

Finally, in relation to the domestic price, we note that this will be highest for the case of VERs and import quotas. The reason is that when these trade barriers are used, the import monopolist faces a fixed upper limit for imports from the discriminated foreign source, A. Therefore, the monopolist will face a lower supply and thereby a higher marginal cost of importing than is the case with a trade policy based on tariffs or social clauses. Accordingly, given the supply from domestic producers and non-discriminated foreign exporters, B, the domestic price will be higher when trade is restricted by means of VERs or import quotas than is the case under a trade policy regime based on social clauses or tariffs.

A Welfare Ranking of Different Discriminatory Trade Barriers

The static effects on prices and quantities have now been analysed with regard to the use of different discriminatory trade policies to restrict imports from a specific country or group of countries. On the basis of this analysis, it is possible to carry out a welfare ranking of the different policies.

The net welfare effect on the importing economy depends on the changes in the consumer surplus, producer surplus, government revenue from the use of trade restrictions and, finally, on changes in the surplus that accrues to the importers of the commodity concerned as a result of the imposition of protectionist measures.

Starting with the consumer surplus, this depends on the domestic price of the commodity. A lower price implies a greater

Figure 4.6: Effects of Discriminatory Policy Means that are Import Equivalent With Regard to Imports from A – the Case of Import Monopoly

Figure 4.6.1: Effects of Discriminatory Social Clauses and Tariffs

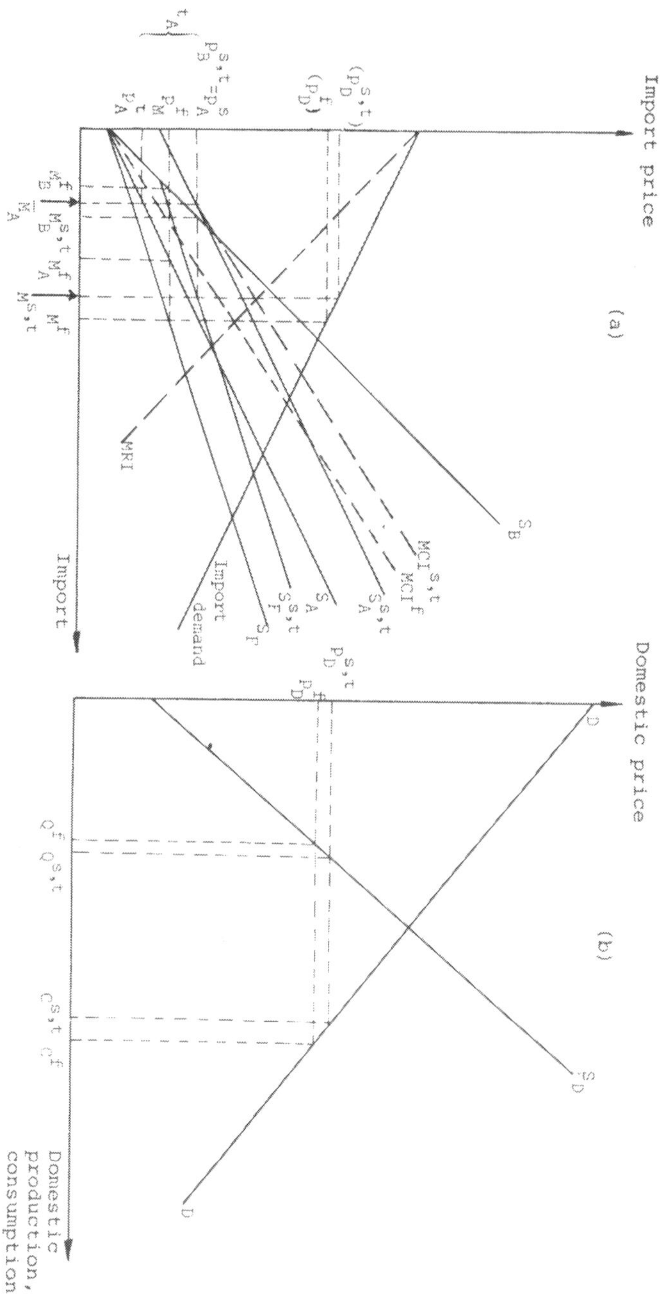

Figure 4.6.2: Effects of Discriminatory Import Quotas and VERS (the results from 4.6.1 are marked on the axes)

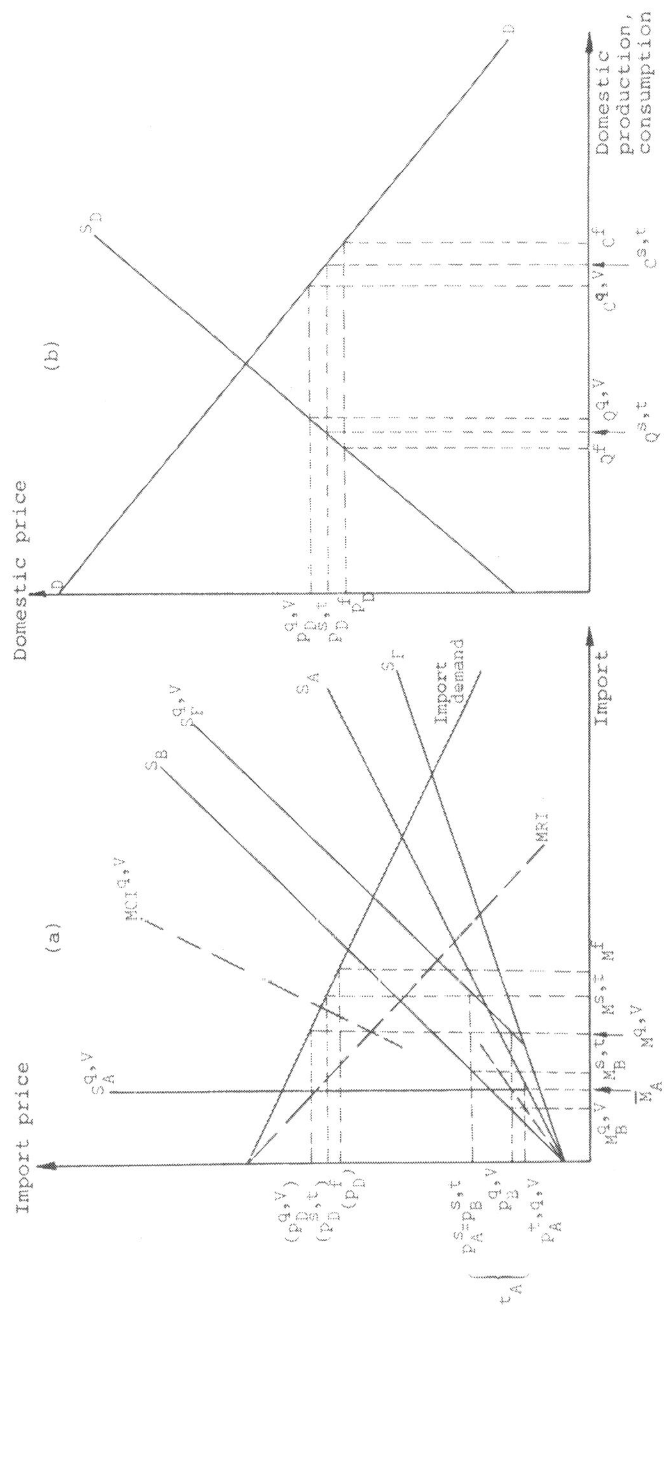

surplus to the consumers. Regarding the surplus to domestic producers, this varies inversely with the consumer surplus. Finally, the government revenue and the surplus to importers both depend on the difference between the domestic and the import price.

Returning to Figure 4.2, we find that in the case of perfect competitive conditions, the consumer and producer surpluses are equivalent for all of the various trade policy measures that have been considered. The differences are to be found in the import activity. In the case of social clauses and VERs there will be no surplus to importers nor any government revenue from importing, whereas in the case of import quotas, importers will obtain a surplus from each unit imported from the discriminated export economy, A, equal to the difference between the domestic price and the import price paid for imports from A. Finally, under a tariff regime, the same surplus will accrue to the government in the importing economy in the form of tariff revenues. Hence, in this case, it can be concluded from a welfare economic point of view, that tariffs and import quotas will be equivalent and superior to social clauses and VERs, which in turn will be equivalent from the static welfare point of view of an importing economy.

By the same procedure, we can derive a welfare ranking also for the other market situations considered. The analysis of an export monopoly in the discriminated export economy or group of economies is straightforward and does not require any comment. In this instance, a tariff will be superior to all of the other policy measures. Furthermore, the various non-tariff barriers that have been analysed will turn out to be equivalent from the static welfare economic point of view of the importing economy.

On the basis of Figures 4.3 and 4.5, it can be concluded that tariffs will be superior to the other trade barriers considered in the cases of monopoly in domestic production and an export monopoly in non-discriminated foreign sources. No other policy instrument produces a lower domestic price, or a lower price paid for imports. In the same way, VERs can be concluded to be inferior to all other policy measures that have been analysed. Regarding the relative ranking of social clauses and import quotas, it is not possible to reach any clear-cut conclusions. On the one hand, social clauses will give rise to a lower domestic price than import quotas. Consequently, the social surplus net of the surplus from importing *per se* will be larger for social clauses than for import quotas. On the other hand, with regard to the surplus that accrues to importers, it can be noted that there will be no such surplus when imports are restricted by means of social clauses, while a surplus will arise when import quotas are used. As a consequence of these differenes, it is not possible to make a unique welfare ranking of social clauses and import quotas when monopoly conditions prevail in either domestic production in the importing economy, or in the export trade of non-discriminated economies.

Finally, in the case of monopoly in the import activity and perfect competition in domestic production and foreign exporting, it is possible to reach a clear-cut and complete welfare ranking of the various measures considered, although this ranking is not as readily apparent as in the case when perfect competition is universal. From Figure 4.6 it is immediately evident that tariffs will be superior to all of the other measures. Furthermore, in this case, import quotas and VERs will be equivalent. From a static welfare economic point of view, social clauses must be superior to these policy measures. First, they give rise to a domestic price below that prevailing under import quotas and VERs. Secondly, the marginal cost of importing will always be lower for social clauses than for import quotas and VERs. Hence, from a static welfare economic point of view, we are now able to summarise, in Table 4.1, an importing economy's ranking of the various trade policy measures that we have analysed.

Table 4.1: Welfare Ranking of Discriminatory Trade Policy Measures that Give Rise to the Same Level of Imports from the Discriminated Foreign Country or Group of Countries

---

The case of perfect competition in domestic production, importing and foreign exporting:

(1) tariff and import quota (equivalent);
(2) social clause and VER (equivalent).

The case of monopoly in domestic production, perfect competition in importing and foreign exporting:

(1) tariff;
(2) import quota or social clause (non-equivalent);
(3) VER.

The case of export monopoly in the discriminated economy, perfect competition in domestic production, importing and in exporting from non-discriminated economies:

(1) tariff;
(2) import quota, VER and social clause (equivalent).

The case of export monopoly in the non-discriminated economy, perfect competition in domestic production, importing and in exporting from discriminated economies:

(1) tariff;
(2) import quota or social clause (non-equivalent);
(3) VER.

The case of monopoly in importing, perfect competition in foreign exporting and domestic production:

(1) tariff;
(2) social clause;
(3) import quota and VER (equivalent).

Summary

From the point of view of an importing economy we have found that the imposition of different trade barriers against a specific export economy, or group of economies, gives rise to effects that can be summarised in Table 4.2 with respect to their equivalences and non-equivalences in relation to prices and quantities.

Discriminatory trade barriers, that are designed to restrict imports from a specific foreign country, or group of countries, by the same amount, have been found to be domestic price- and output-equivalent when perfect competition prevails in the importing country's domestic production and import activities and in export trade in non-discriminated foreign countries. In these cases, the measures considered will also be equivalent with regard to the total level of imports and the price paid for imports from non-discriminated foreign sources. We have also found that among the different policy measures, there are no measures that will give rise to a higher price for imports from discriminated countries than the social clause, with the exception of the cases of a monopoly in domestic production in the importing economy or in the export trade of non-discriminated foreign sources. In these cases a VER gives rise to an even higher price.

Finally, if we rank the different trade policy measures from the point of view of the importing country's welfare, tariffs were

Table 4.2: Equivalences of Discriminatory Policy Measures Under Different Market Conditions

	Discriminatory Policy Means that are Import-equivalent Concerning Imported Quantity from A and also are Equivalent with Respect to:		
Market Conditions	Domestic Price and Output	Price Paid for Imports from A	Price Paid for Imports from B, Import Quantity from B and Total Import
Perfect competition in domestic production, importing and foreign exporting	Social clauses, tariffs, import quotas and VERs	Social clauses and VERS; tariffs and import quotas	Social clauses tariffs, import quotas and VERs
Monopoly in domestic production. Perfect competition in importing and foreign exporting	Import quotas and VERs	Tariffs and import quotas	Import quotas and VERs
Monopoly in importing. Perfect competition in domestic production and foreign exporting	Import quotas and VERs	Tariffs, import quotas and VERs	Import quotas and VERs
Monopoly in exporting in A. Perfect competition in domestic production, importing and exporting in B	Social clauses, tariffs, import quotas and VERs	Social clauses, import quotas and VERs	Social clauses, tariffs, import quotas and VERs
Monopoly in exporting in B. Perfect competition in domestic production importing and exporting in A	Import quotas and VERs	Tariffs and import quotas	Import quotas and VERs

Note: 1. A, Discriminated Economies and B, Non-discriminated Economies.

found to be superior to all the other measures, while social clauses will never be inferior to VERs.[6] The ranking of social clauses and import quotas depends on the market conditions at hand. In the case of perfect competition in domestic production as well as in importing and foreign exporting, import quotas will be superior to social clauses, whereas social clauses will be superior to import quotas when there is a monopoly in importing and perfect competition in foreign exporting and domestic production.

4.3 Comparative Trade Policy Analysis – The Discriminated Exporting Economy

In the preceding section we have found that, as a rule, protective social clauses will not be rejected as an alternative to import quotas or VERs by welfare maximising import economies that wish to restrict imports from a specific foreign country or group of countries. On the basis of the analysis in the previous section, we may also conclude that a non-discriminated foreign country, with regard to the surplus of 'clause-covered' commodities, will prefer import quotas and VERs to tariffs and social clauses, or be indifferent between the various measures, under all market conditions considered in section 4.2 with the exception of the case of an import monopoly in the importing economy. Furthermore, it is clear, from the definition of the social clause, that this type of policy gives the export economies concerned the possibility to choose between:

(a) a change in working conditions (in this case the social clauses are said to be efficient); and
(b) unchanged working conditions which may give rise to trade barriers being imposed upon manufacturing exports that have been produced by means of substandard working conditions.

Consequently, from the point of view of export economies covered by social clauses, there can be no economic arguments against an introduction of such clauses, unless this brings about an increase in the degree of protectionism facing the economies concerned. However, the effects of the introduction of social clauses on working conditions in export economies that do not comply with the requirements stated in the clauses remains an important issue. Hitherto, it has been assumed that social clauses are effective, i.e. the introduction of social clauses gives rise to changes in working conditions that fulfil the requirements of the clauses. Let us now examine this assumption in greater detail by comparing the effects of such changes with the effects that arise out of VERs and foreign imposed tariffs and import quotas, in order to find out whether, and under what circumstances, social clauses can be expected to be efficient.

The Choice For a Small Country

In Chapter 3, it was found that the production possibilities and national income would be reduced when social clauses gave rise to changes in working conditions in order to comply with the requirements of the clauses. This finding was based on the small country assumption of an individual export economy. This would be valid for all types of protective social clauses. If, on the other hand, the country takes no actions to satisfy the labour standard requirements of the clauses, it would be confronted with other types of trade barriers. Given the small country assumption, a self-imposed VER will be clearly preferred to social clauses, tariffs and import quotas, by an export economy that wishes to maximise its national income. Contrary to social clauses VERs, import quotas and tariffs do not give rise to a reduction of production possibilities. Furthermore, given the small country assumption, the price paid for exported commodities will be unaffected since a VER is assumed to be imposed and administered by the export economy itself, i.e. the quotas are distributed in the export economy. Regarding foreign-imposed tariffs and import quotas, these will affect the export economy in the same way as a reduction in the demand for the economy's manufacturing exports. Consequently, the imposition of these measures will be equivalent to an exogenous reduction of the price of manufactures. Hence, it can be concluded that from a national income point of view, these traditional policy measures will be inferior to an export equivalent VER.

However, it is not possible to derive such a ranking for export equivalent and efficient social clauses on the one hand, and tariffs and import quotas on the other. In the case of efficient social clauses, the production possibilities of the economy concerned will be reduced, whereas foreign-imposed tariffs and import quotas do not give rise to such a reduction, but lead to a reduction of the national income as a result of the lower price paid for manufacturing exports from the economy.

Finally, we note that as long as the small country assumption is satisfied, export equivalent tariffs and import quotas will have an equivalent effect on national income in the export economy concerned. Hence, it may be concluded that an export economy that cannot influence international prices and that faces a choice between export equivalent VERs and foreign-imposed efficient social clauses, tariffs and import quotas, will prefer VERs, and be indifferent between tariffs and import quotas whereas the ranking of efficient social clauses on the one hand, and tariffs and import quotas on the other, will be indeterminate. Consequently, VERs will always be chosen from a national income point of view when there is the possibility of avoiding foreign imposed barriers. In this case social clauses cannot be expected to be efficient. However, if social clauses are designed so that the alternative to changes in working conditions is a tariff or an import quota, we cannot be certain of the incapacity of social clauses as a means to change working conditions.

The Choice When International Prices are not Exogenously Given

The analysis becomes considerably more complicated if we remove the small country assumption and assume that the social clauses are not only directed against manufacturing exports from a minor export economy but against a large proportion of the exporters in question. Changes in trade policy would then affect the international price of manufactures.

First, let us recall some of the results derived in section 4.2:

(i) in all market situations considered, efficient social clauses will raise the international price, while the use of discriminatory and import equivalent tariffs and, as a rule, also import quotas, will lower this price. VERs will raise the price in all market situations except the case of monopoly in importing.

(ii) social clauses and VERs will be equivalent with regard to the price paid for imports from the discriminated economy, or group of economies, as long as importing and domestic production in the importing economy and exporting in non-discriminated economies are characterised by perfect competition. In the case of monopoly in importing, a social clause will give rise to a price above the price that will arise out of a VER, while the opposite holds for the case of monopoly in domestic production, and the case of export monopoly in non-discriminated economies.

Consequently, the export economy considered will obtain higher earnings from manufacturing exports when it faces an external trade policy based on VERs or social clauses, than in the case when it faces an export equivalent external trade policy based on tariffs or import quotas. In fact, export equivalent VERs and efficient social clauses will also be equivalent with respect to manufacturing export earnings, as long as domestic production and importing in the importing economy and exporting in non-discriminated economies are characterised by perfect competition. In the cases of monopoly in domestic production and in exporting in non-discriminated economies, a VER will give rise to the largest export revenues, while in the case of a monopoly in importing, social clauses will take this position.

Accordingly, an attempt will now be made to rank the different policy measures with respect to their effect on national income once the small country assumption has been removed. First, VERs will always give rise to a higher, or at least as high a level of national income as export equivalent tariffs or import quotas.

If manufactures are assumed to be the only commodities, the price of which is affected by the analysed trade policy changes, it can be concluded that an export economy, within the group of discriminated economies, confronted with a choice between the different export equivalent measures considered, would prefer VERs to tariffs and import quotas. Moreover, as long as there is no import monopoly in the importing economy VERs would be preferred to social clauses as well.

The terms of trade must change in the same direction as the price of manufactures since the price on manufactures has been assumed to be the only price affected by the policy changes. As we have found previously, VERs lead to an increase in the international price level in all cases with the exception of the case of an import monopoly in the importing economy. Furthermore, in this latter case a VER does not give rise to a price lower than that arising out of a foreign export equivalent tariff or import quota regime directed against the export economy in question. Accordingly, VERs must result in a level of national income which is at least as high as that associated with the other two measures. With regard to the ranking of export equivalent VERs and efficient social clauses, we know that these measures will give rise to the same price of manufactures as long as there is perfect competition in domestic production and importing in the importing economy as well as in exporting in non-discriminated foreign sources. Furthermore, VERs have been found to give rise to a higher price level than social clauses when a domestic production monopoly exists in the importing economy, or there is a monopoly in exporting in non-discriminated export economies. Since we also know that social clauses give rise to a reduction of the economy's production possibilities, it follows that VERs are superior to efficient social clauses in terms of the discriminated export economy's national income in all market situations considered except the case of monopoly in importing.

By the same line of reasoning, we may conclude that, as a rule, import quotas will be preferred to export equivalent tariffs, whereas the ranking of efficient social clauses on the one hand, and tariffs and import quotas on the other, will be indeterminate. Finally, in the case of an import monopoly in the importing economy, the ranking of export equivalent VERs and efficient social clauses will also be indeterminate.

A comparison between the national income effects of export equivalent social clauses and VERs will also result in an indeterminate outcome when the prices of both manufactures and non-manufacturing goods may change due to the analysed trade policy changes. This is due to the greater uncertainty regarding the terms of trade effects of the two measures compared with the case when only the price of manufactures is affected.

The Choice from a Group Interest Point of View

Due to the difficulties in ranking social clauses and traditional trade barriers from the standpoint of a discriminated exporting economy's national income, we will analyse the effects on factor rewards, in order to find out whether it is possible to draw any conclusions with regard to the political pressure for different measures in an export economy that has to choose between efficient social clauses and export equivalent traditional trade barriers.

In the case of foreign imposed tariffs directed against manufacturing exports, we have found that the price of manufactures will decrease in all market situations. This will also be true for the case of import quotas, except when there is a monopoly in exporting. Furthermore, we have found that, as a rule, VERs will give rise to an increase in the international price of manufactures. However, in this case, the reduction in supply has not been caused by any cost or price factors. Therefore, with VERs, exported manufactures will give the export quota holders, or the government in the export economy, a rent. The only market situation, of those considered in the present study, in which VERs will not give rise to a higher price and an export rent is the case of import monopoly in the importing economy. Besides the effects on the rents from exporting, VERs will give rise to the same effects on resource allocation in the exporting economies as foreign-imposed and export equivalent tariffs and import quotas.

Regarding factor rewards, traditional trade barriers will give rise to clear-cut effects in labour surplus economies. Wages and the return to land will be unaffected, whereas the incomes of mineowners will increase, and the return to capital decrease. Even if wages remain unaffected, we note that this type of trade policy action easily will give rise to negative effects on the workers. The number of employees in the formal parts of the economy will decrease in the short run. This decrease will continue during the economy's path to a new long run equilibrium, provided that manufacturing is the labour intensive industry.[7]

In a full employment economy, wages will be negatively affected by the imposition of traditional trade barriers against manufacturing exports, provided that manufacturing is the labour-intensive industry. A reduction in wages will increase the returns to land due to the increase in agricultural employment. The effect on the return to capital will be indeterminate, whereas mineowners will receive increased incomes due to the expansion of the extractive industry.[8]

If we turn to the effects on factor rewards of efficient social clauses, we have found in Chapter 3 that at constant commodity prices, the effects on the incomes of owners of land and mines will generally be in the same direction as when traditional trade barriers are used to restrict manufacturing exports. Furthermore, the long run effects on the return to capital were found to be indeterminate in full employment economies and negative in labour surplus economies. It was also found that, as a rule, the introduction of efficient social clauses would give rise to an income redistribution between workers who are employed in manufacturing and workers outside this industry. The redistribution takes the following form. When working conditions are changed in manufacturing, these changes will be 'paid' by workers who are now outside this industry. Since manufacturing employment is, as a rule, negatively affected by the changes in working conditions, non-manufacturing wages tend to decrease in full employment economies, whereas in labour surplus economies, the employment in the formal parts of the economy tends to be reduced.

Removing the assumption of constant commodity prices, we have found that efficient social clauses will always increase the international price of manufactures. Hence, the effects on factor rewards and income distribution between different categories of workers, that we have derived in Chapter 3, will be weakened. Consequently, in the case of efficient social clauses covering a sufficiently large proportion of the international supply of manufactures, another form of 'financing' the changes in the manufacturing working conditions becomes evident. The type of 'rent' that arises from exporting under a VER regime will in this case accrue to workers who are employed in manufacturing after the changes in working conditions. Therefore, it is important to note that with a trade policy based on social clauses, there is a possibility that at least some workers are made better off, especially in a short-run perspective, whereas no such possibility exists when traditional trade barriers are used. Consequently, from a political economy standpoint, it can be concluded that in the context of a trade policy that includes social clauses, manufacturing workers would tend to prefer changes in working conditions in order to satisfy the requirements of the clauses rather than a regime of restricted manufacturing exports due to foreign imposed tariffs or import quotas. Social clauses tend also to be preferred to self-imposed VERs given that these are not combined with an income redistribution scheme that is favourable for these workers.

Summary

From a national income point of view, a discriminated export economy can be expected to prefer VERs to export equivalent tariffs, import quotas and social clauses. No clear-cut ranking has been found with regard to the effects on national income of social clauses on the one hand and tariffs and import quotas on the other. However, from a political economy point of view we have found that manufacturing workers tend to be in favour of social clauses.

4.4 Concluding Remarks

In this chapter, we have compared the economic effects of protective social clauses with the effects of discriminatory tariffs, import quotas and 'voluntary' export restraints (VERs), that give rise to the same import from a specific foreign source. We have found that:

(1) In all market situations considered, protective and efficient social clauses will raise the price paid for imports from the export economy or group of economies covered by social clauses, whereas the use of discriminatory and import equivalent tariffs and, as a rule also import quotas, will lower this price. Finally, VERs have been found to raise this price in all market situations considered except the case of monopoly in importing.

(2) Social clauses and VERs will be equivalent with regard to the price paid for imports from the discriminated economy, or group of economies, provided that importing and domestic production in the importing economy and exporting in non-discriminated economies are characterised by perfect competition. In the case of monopoly in importing, a social clause will give rise to a price above the price that would have arisen from a VER, while the opposite would be the result in the case of a monopoly in domestic production and in the case of an export monopoly in non-discriminated economies.

(3) From the static welfare economic point of view of an importing economy, tariffs will be preferred to social clauses as well as to the other means considered, whereas social clauses will never be inferior to VERs. The welfare ranking of social clauses and import quotas depends critically on the market situation in foreign exporting and in importing and domestic production in the importing economy.

(4) In relation to the surplus from exporting the 'clause-covered' commodity, a non-discriminated export economy prefers VERs and import quotas to social clauses and tariffs, or is indifferent between the various trade barriers in question,

in all market situations considered except the case when there is an import monopoly in the importing economy.

(5) From the standpoint of a discriminated export economy's national income, VERs will never be inferior to export equivalent tariffs and import quotas. Provided that only the price of the discriminated commodity is affected and that importing in the import economy is characterised by perfect competition, VERs will also be preferred to social clauses. Furthermore, we have found that there is no such clear-cut ranking of social clauses on the one hand and tariffs and import quotas on the other.

(6) Workers in the foreign industry covered by the social clauses tend to prefer efficient social clauses to tariffs and different forms of quotas. This is especially the case in labour surplus economies and when short run effects are given high priority.

(7) In order to maximise the likelihood that social clauses will be efficient, these clauses should be designed in such a manner that if necessary changes in working conditions are not made, a tariff will face the exports of 'clause-covered' commodities.

Before we conclude this chapter, some final comments will be made. Let us disregard existing agreements and rules of international trade. We can then recall one of our conclusions in section 3.7, where it was stated that an export economy, confronted with a social clause on wages, has the possibility to change working conditions so that the requirements of the clause become satisfied and by means of appropriate factor tax-cum-subsidies re-establish the initial production mix, without running into problems in the international market. In the light of this alternative, changes in working conditions that are made in order to comply with the requirements of this clause become more likely since the national income remains unaffected. On the other hand, the failure to make such changes will give rise to problems for manufacturing exports, and thereby the national income. This conclusion is valid for the case when social clauses are directed against exports from economies that take international prices as exogenously given, as well as in the case when this small country assumption is not satisfied.

We should also note that an efficient incorporation of social clauses in the rules that govern international trade may give the discriminated export economies a sort of monopoly power in trade, if these countries are considered as a unity. If social clauses are introduced and efficiently supervised, i.e. non-compliance is met by trade barriers that restrict exports of non-complying economies at least as much as had been the case if the necessary changes in working conditions had been made, the international price and thereby also the export revenues may well increase so much that the national income increases.

One may ask why the same export economies do not join together today so that the same fruits can be taken without making any sacrifices with regard to their production possibilities. This question is quite easy to answer by referring to the well-known problem of keeping cartels intact, without imposing numerous costs on their members for controlling each other's actions. If, for instance, a group of countries exporting a certain commodity join together in a cartel that decides to restrict exports and obtain monopoly profits, there will always be a tendency for an individual member to increase its profits from the trade in question by breaking the agreement. This phenomenon is very frequent in all types of collective activities that rely on the restrictive practices of the individual members of the collective, and is known as the *prisoner's dilemma*.

Even if there exist some successful cartels of this kind in international markets, of which the best known in the 1970s has been the oil producer cartel OPEC, it would seem unrealistic to suggest a successful cartel of countries in the world market for manufactures. One reason is simply the great number of potential exporters of manufactured goods among less developed countries. In the case of oil and other raw materials where cartels have been successful, the number of members and potential members has been relatively low. Consequently, the cartel has come to cover a sufficiently large proportion of the world market supply of the commodity in question to make the cartel profitable. By an efficient introduction of social clauses in international trade relations, it may be possible to obtain the same effects as those arising out of an efficient cartel.

Notes

1. The previous works in this field can be classified into at least the following three groups:

(a) Static partial analyses of equivalences, see e.g. Bergsten (1975), Bhagwati (1965, 1968), Shibata (1968), Takacs (1978) and Yadav (1968).
(b) Equivalences and non-equivalences under uncertainty, see e.g. Fishelson and Flatters (1975), Kreinin (1970), Pelcovits (1976), Vastrup (1979) and Walter (1971).
(c) Equivalences and non-equivalences under retaliation, see e.g. Rodrigues (1974) and Tower (1975).

2. Bhagwati (1965).
3. McCulloch (1973).
4. Bergsten (1975), p. 240.
5. This figure can be found in Takacs (1978). Takacs' article effectively summarises the previous work on static equivalences and non-equivalences between import equivalent and non-discriminatory tariffs and quotas. Takacs also completes the previous studies by analysing the equivalences and non-equivalences between non-discriminatory import equivalent tariffs and import quotas on the one hand and non-discriminatory as well as discriminatory VERs on the other. In our analyses we concentrate on equivalences and non-equivalences between various discriminatory trade policy measures.
6. This will also be true when the policy measures are designed so that they give rise to the same total import to the protective economy, with the exception of the case of monopoly in importing. From Table 4.2 it is clear that in the cases when perfect competition prevails in the importing economy's domestic production and import activities, and in export trade in non-discriminated foreign sources, policy measures that are import equivalent with respect to imports from a specific foreign economy are also equivalent in relation to total imports.

For the case of monopoly in domestic production, it can be demonstrated that protective social clauses will be superior to totally import equivalent VERs from the importing economy's static welfare point of view. The reason is that VERs will give rise to a higher domestic price than social clauses since the foreign supply curve that faces the importing economy is steeper in the case of VERs than in the case of social clauses.

Turning to the case of export monopoly in non-discriminated foreign sources, totally import equivalent social clauses and VERs will also be equivalent from an importing economy's static welfare point of view. The reason is that, in this case, total import equivalence between social clauses and VERs implies import price equivalence, domestic output equivalence and thereby also domestic price equivalence.

Finally, in the case of import monopoly, social clauses can be demonstrated to be inferior to totally import equivalent VERs, since social clauses give rise to higher import prices than VERs.

By an analogous analysis it can be demonstrated that social clauses are inferior to domestic *output equivalent* VERs only in the case of import monopoly in the protective economy.

7. These effects have been derived by the same method as was used in Chapter 3. By solving the system of equations that relates to a labour surplus economy for short run effects on factor rewards when the price of manufactures changes we obtain: $dr_M/dp_M = M/K_M > O$, whereas other factor rewards are unaffected.

Consequently, in the longer run capital will move out of manufacturing. For the effects on factor rewards during this reallocation of capital, see Table 3.6.

8. These effects have been derived from the system of equations in section 3.2 that relates to a full employment economy. By solving this system of equations for the short run effects on factor rewards when the price of manufactures changes we obtain:

$$dw/dp_M = (1/D)p_E E_{LL} A_{LL} M_L > 0$$
$$dv/dp_M = (1/D)p_E E_{LL} A_{RL} M_L < 0$$
$$dr/_M/dp_M = (1/D)[p_E E_{LL} A_{LL} M_K - p_M(M_{LK} M/L_M)(p_E E_{LL} + A_{LL})] > 0$$
$$dr_E/dp_M = (1/D)p_E E_{KL} A_{LL} M_L < 0$$

where

$$D = p_E E_{LL} A_{LL} + p_M M_{LL}(p_E E_{LL} + A_{LL}) > 0$$

In the longer run capital will be reallocated from manufacturing to the extractive industry as a consequence of the reduced price of manufactures. For the effects on factor rewards during this reallocation, see Table 3.9.

5 SUMMARY AND POLICY CONSIDERATIONS

5.1 Introduction

In this chapter we sum up the results of the previous analyses and take a closer look at their policy implications. We will also comment on some practical aspects of incorporating social clauses in the rules that govern international trade.

We begin by noting that the question of international labour standards and trade has more than a century-long history. The awareness of the relationship between labour standards and international competitiveness was also one of the major bases for the formation of the International Labour Organisation (ILO) in 1919. In the Preamble to the ILO Constitution it is explicitly stated that 'the failure of any nation to adopt human conditions of labour is an obstacle in the way of other nations which desire to improve the conditions in their own countries'.[1]

Notwithstanding the formation of the ILO and the important work on improving working conditions that has been carried out inside this organisation, the question of the introduction of labour standards in trade policy has continued to be subject of debate. In the last decade, proposals for incorporating a social clause or labour standards in the General Agreement on Tariffs and Trade (GATT) have been advanced frequently in the trade policy debate.

The incorporation of a social clause in the rules governing international trade would force the countries that do not comply with the minimum labour standard requirements of the claûse to choose between a change in their working conditions, or to run the risk of being confronted with an increase in traditional trade barriers in the international markets for those commodities that are produced by means of substandard working conditions.

To a large extent, the debate on the incorporation of social clauses in international trade relations has centred around the aims that have been thought to underlie the incorporation of such clauses. The following aims have been advanced:

(1) To provide protection to domestic industries and workers in the 'old' industrial countries.
(2) To represent an action of solidarity with workers that now

are working under 'unacceptably low' working conditions.

(3) To protect the international 'free trade system' from increased protectionism based on traditional trade barriers.

Let us sum up the results of our analysis by starting out from each of these aims.

5.2 Summary of Analytical Results

Social Clauses and Protectionism

If social clauses are to provide protection to domestic industries in the 'old' industrial countries, the clauses must result in an increased price being paid for imports of commodities covered by the social clauses. This will only happen when the clauses in question are cost increasing and the export economies that are required to change their working conditions are responsible for a sufficiently large proportion of the imports of the commodity in question in the importing, protectionist economies. In other cases, the social clauses will not give rise to any price effects. Consequently, social clauses cannot be expected to protect domestic industries in cases when the foreign producers, who do not comply with the minimum requirements included in the clauses, are so small that as a group they have no influence on the international price of the commodity in question. Therefore, if protection is the main aim, there are other more efficient measures to be found in the arsenal of traditional trade barriers. Furthermore, it is important to note that from an economic welfare point of view, various tax-cum-subsidy programmes are superior to trade policy measures when the aim of the policy is to protect domestic industries.

Social Clauses and Solidarity

With regard to the argument that social clauses should be seen as actions of solidarity with workers who are at present working under 'unacceptably low' working conditions, this is not primarily a question of the proportion of the international market held by the export economies directly affected by the clauses but of the relative size of the importing, protectionist economies in that market, the character of the clause and also the factor market characteristics of the export economies concerned.

It is obvious that if a small importing economy introduces a social clause in its trade relations, the effects on foreign working conditions will be very limited. However, if social clauses are introduced in GATT and really become efficient, workers in economies with substandard working conditions will clearly be affected. The form taken by the changes of working conditions will depend on the character of the incorporated clauses and the factor market characteristics of the clause-covered export economies.

The effects of a clause that demands basic trade union rights for foreign workers who do not have such rights are not entirely clear. A clause of this type may result in a great variety of union activities. As this type of social clause entitles workers to determine how to use their basic trade union rights, an efficient incorporation of the clause can clearly be classified as an action of solidarity with workers in economies where such basic rights do not exist.

Turning to social clauses on specific working conditions, we begin by retaining the assumption from Chapter 3 of given and constant international commodity prices. By this assumption we isolate the question as to whether different social clauses on specific working conditions can be viewed as general actions of solidarity when the export economies in question, taken as a group, satisfy the small country assumption.

One important and frequently emphasised aspect of working life is the wage level. The introduction of a social clause on wages, that demands a certain minimum wage level in the manufacturing export industry, will raise wages for workers employed in this industry in countries where the current wages are too low. Consequently, a social clause on wages can be clearly seen as an action of solidarity with workers who remain employed in the foreign export industry that had been forced to raise wages by the imposition of the social clause. However, this is not the complete story of how foreign workers are affected by the introduction of this type of clause. As a rule, the increased number of foreign workers outside the manufacturing export industry will find themselves worse off after the incorporation of such a clause. In full employment economies, the negative effect will consist of lower wages, whereas in labour surplus economies there will be a decrease in employment in the formal sectors. Therefore, in a more complete perspective, a social clause that demands minimum wages for workers in the manufacturing industry is a doubtful means of solidarity with foreign workers.

As far as social clauses on hours of work and child labour are concerned, they would also seem to be of doubtful effect from the point of view of solidarity with foreign workers. These types of clauses do not affect production in labour surplus economies. Nevertheless, in the case of a clause on child labour, the resultant income redistribution may be detrimental to large size families. However, the negative effects for this type of family should be weighed against the potential gains for child welfare that can arise from a reduction in child labour. By complementary social and educational policy actions, a clause on child labour can pave the way for a more complete general prohibition of child labour without having a negative effect on large size families. Consequently, in this broader perspective, the clause on child labour can be said to show signs of solidarity with workers in economies that permit children to employed in their export industry.

Also in the case of full employment economies it is uncertain whether social clauses on child labour and hours of work will really have an effect on production. As a rule, the clause on hours of work can be expected to give rise to a migration of labour between different firms or sectors of production, leaving the output mix unaffected. This may also be the case for a social clause on child labour. Production will be affected by the clause on hours of work when a wage differential emerges in favour of workers in the industry covered by the clause. It should be noted in this context that even if the workers who remain in this industry after the introduction of the clause receive higher hourly wages in the short run, it cannot be stated with certainty that they are better off than before. First, in the longer run, there is a risk that hourly wages will decrease not only for workers outside the 'clause-covered' industry, but also for workers within this industry. Secondly, even if hourly wages for workers in the export industry are really positively affected by the clause, we cannot be sure that they prefer the new mix of hours of work and totally received wages.

With regard to the case when the clause on child labour gives rise to production effects, the wages for adult labour will be positively affected whereas there will be a fall in the wages of working children. Consequently, we can conclude that this type of social clause may also be detrimental for large size families in full employment economies.

Finally, we have also analysed the effects of introducing a social clause on occupational health and safety. Besides the clause on basic trade union rights, this type of social clause has the most imprecise character of the claues considered in this study.

Consequently, it is also difficult to predict its likely effects. However, in section 3.6 we have analysed the effects of necessary changes in the manufacturing working environment by assuming that such changes can be characterised as negative technical changes. Using that approach we found it possible to derive certain conclusions that have an important bearing on how foreign workers will be affected.

According to our analysis in labour surplus economies, employment in the formal sectors will decrease, whereas workers who remain employed in the manufacturing export industry, following the changes in the working environment, will clearly be better off than prior to the changes. This conclusion cannot be made for full employment economies. In this type of economy, there is a risk that the real wage in manufacturing, as well as in other sectors of the economy, will decrease due to the changes in working environment that have to be made in order to satisfy the minimum requirements of the clause.

The overall conclusion regarding the question of social clauses as measures of solidarity is that, in relation to the total labour force, social clauses on specific working conditions are of dubious value. Restricting the perspective to those workers who remain employed in the manufacturing export industry following the introduction of the clauses and the necessary changes in working conditions, it has been found that with the exception of the clause on hours of work, these workers will never be made worse off in labour surplus economies. However, this type of statement cannot be made in relation to full employment economies.

These conclusions have been derived from the assumption that the social clauses have been introduced without having any effects on the use of other trade barriers or on the international price of the commodity covered by the clauses. However, in Chapter 4, we have compared the economic effects of using different traditional trade barriers with those that arise from the use of social clauses in trade policy. From that analysis, important differences were found in relation to the effects on workers in 'clause-covered' export economies when different external trade policy measures are used.

Benefits will accrue to workers who continue to be employed in the manufacturing export industry following the introduction of the social clauses. If we take potential effects on the international price of manufactures into consideration in our analysis of social clauses, the negative effects associated with the clauses will be reduced without at the same time diminishing the positive effects, provided that the covered manufacturing industry is the labour-intensive industry. No positive effects on the situation of foreign workers were found when other trade barriers were used to restrict the imports from economies that are required to change their working conditions due to the introduction of social clauses. These types of trade policy measures result in decreased real wages in full employment economies and decreased employment in the formal parts of labour surplus economies. Consequently, in terms of a comparison of various trade policy measures, it is easier to find solidarity in relation to social clauses than when such clauses are introduced under an assumption of *ceteris paribus*. However, as a general rule, only the social clause on basic trade union rights can be classified as a means of solidarity with foreign workers.

Social Clauses and Traditional Protectionism

Looking at the real world, we find that increased industrial exports from developing countries have been frequently met by different types of trade barriers in the old industrial world. In cases when the increased demand and use of trade barriers against imports of industrial goods from developing countries are based on what are considered to be unfair working conditions, it is obvious that the basis for traditional protectionism will be reduced or even disappear once working conditions are actually altered to comply with the requirements of the social clauses. In cases where no such arguments are presented for the increased use of trade barriers against imports of industrial goods from developing countries, the cost increases, that as a rule arise from the changes in working conditions, will reduce the competitiveness of these countries. Thereby the use of traditional trade barriers will also be reduced, *ceteris paribus*.

From this reasoning it can be concluded that social clauses will protect the international trade system against increased protectionism based on traditional trade barriers. However, in order to be used as an argument in favour of social clauses, this type of trade policy measure must be proved to be superior to trade barriers at work today, given the aims of the policy.

One difference between the two sets of trade policy measures has already been dealt with in the section on social clauses and solidarity. It was concluded there that a clause on basic trade union rights can clearly be classified as a measure of solidarity with foreign workers who do not have such rights, whereas the clauses on specific working conditions were found to be more doubtful from this point of view. Nevertheless, such clauses also have some beneficial effects for foreign workers whereas traditional trade barriers do not, provided that the export industry covered by the clauses is labour-intensive. We have also concluded that if social clauses are used in trade policy, there will be less room for achieving international competitiveness by worsening working conditions.

Furthermore, in Chapter 4 we have found that from the importing economies static welfare economic point of view, social clauses will be preferred to VERs in all market situations considered. On the other hand, tariffs will always be preferred to social clauses. These findings clearly give us one explanation for the resistance to social clauses, or labour standards in trade policy, during the period when tariffs dominated among trade policy measures. However, according to Bergsten, and the literature on the increased protectionism of the 1970s VERs have come to play an increasing role in the international trade policy since the early 1960s.[2] At first glance, this may seem a bit confusing if we consider the findings of this study.

However, we should remember that social clauses have a distinct character of interfering with other countries' domestic relations, while VERs do not since they are negotiated and formally applied by the exporting countries. Furthermore, we should not forget that in the absence of tariffs, which for manufacturing goods have been negotiated away by the work of GATT during the post-war period, VERs, which lie outside the scope of this organisation, provide an attractive method of seeking protection without running into open conflict with the commitments made inside GATT. We should also observe that the tariffs that would have been required in order to reach the same protection as is now guaranteed by the VERs, would have been so high as to be politically unacceptable. Moreover, a tariff policy inside GATT requires non-discrimination as well as reciprocity. To keep established relations with old trading partners, discriminatory policy measures become attractive when demands for the protection of domestic production have been raised. If VERs are used, there is no explicit claim for reciprocity. Furthermore, discrimination is a central feature of this policy. Finally, it should be kept in mind that as VERs are quotas, they provide domestic producers in the importing economy with a greater producer surplus as well as more secure protection than was the case when tariffs were used.

From the above reasoning it is more easy to understand why the politicians of the old industrial world have relied so heavily on VERs during the 1970s. However, even if we neglect the general problems of protectionism, the increased use of VERs is very problematic from the point of view of the international allocation of resources.

A policy based on VERs will inevitably involve a greater degree of uncertainty than is the case when protectionism is based on tariffs. As VERs works outside a well defined and accepted set of rules, like GATT, it is difficult to predict when and how the policy will be used. Therefore, together with its discriminatory character, VERs increase the degree of uncertainty for investors and producers in comparison with a situation where trade policy is based on tariffs.

Many of the negative effects connected with VERs would disappear if VERs were replaced by a trade policy including social clauses, since efficient social clauses have great similarities with tariffs in that they both work through the price system. Even if social clauses are discriminatory with respect to working conditions, they are non-discriminatory in all other respects. Therefore, given the requirements on working conditions, the clauses will not discriminate against the most efficient producers as is often the case under a trade policy regime based on VERs.

In short, the incorporation of social clauses in the rules that govern international trade can be expected to reduce the extent of traditional protectionism. The question as to whether this is a favourable or unfavourable development depends upon the angle from which it is viewed. Social clauses can be expected to benefit at least some foreign workers now employed under poor working conditions if compared to the effects that will arise out of the use of traditional trade barriers, *ceteris paribus*. From the standpoint of the national income of the exporting economy covered by the clause, VERs will be preferred to social clauses, while from the point of view of the importing economies' static economic welfare, the opposite will be true. Finally, from an international resource allocation perspective, a change in trade policy away from VERs towards a policy including social clauses will give rise to important positive effects.

Summary

In this section, we have summarised the results of our analysis by relating them to the different aims that have been advanced in the debate on introducing labour standards in trade policy. In brief we have found that:

(a) To give protection to domestic industries in the 'old' industrial world, the enforced clause should:
  (i) be cost increasing;
  (ii) cover a sufficiently large proportion of the exporters to the 'old' industrial world so that the import price will be affected.

(b) To be a general measure of solidarity with foreign workers who are at present working under what is defined as 'unacceptably low' working conditions, the enforced clause should:
  (i) be enforced by a sufficiently large proportion of the importing economies in order that working conditions in foreign export industries, that now are 'unacceptable', will be improved;
  (ii) not by itself give rise to negative effects on the situation of workers who are outside the covered export industry after the introduction of the social clause.

(c) To give protection to the international 'free trade system' against increased protectionism based on traditional trade barriers, the enforced clause should:
  (i) remove arguments of 'unfair' competition that are now advanced as arguments for existing or proposed traditional trade barriers; or
  (ii) be cost increasing.

Relating the different types of social clauses that have been analysed to the above conditions, we may conclude that:

(1) A *world-wide* clause on basic trade union rights will satisfy the conditions for social clauses as measures of solidarity and clauses as a means of protecting the 'free trade system' against increased traditional protectionism.

(2) A *world-wide* clause on hours of work or child labour will satisfy the conditions for social clauses as a means to protect the 'free trade system' against increased traditional protectionism.

Only under certain conditions do these clauses satisfy the conditions for social clauses to give protection to domestic industries in the old industrial world. It should be noted that if the covered export economies can be characterised as labour surplus economies these clauses will never have a protective effect.

(3) A *world-wide* clause on wages, and generally the clause on occupational health and safety will satisfy the conditions for clauses to give protection to domestic industries in the old industrial world, and also for clauses to be a means of protecting the 'free trade system' against increased traditional protectionism.

5.3 Social Clauses and GATT

In the previous section, we concluded that if social clauses are to be introduced in trade policy and are to satisfy the different aims that have been advanced in the debate, they should be introduced in a world-wide manner. Furthermore, we have noted that there would be much to gain if trade policy could be brought back to the supervision of GATT. We will now relate the question of social clauses to the existing General Agreement on Tariffs and Trade. Can labour standards be interpreted in the existing agreement? How can such standards explicitly be incorporated in the agreement and, finally, which labour standards should be incorporated?

Interpreting Labour Standards in the Existing GATT

As mentioned in Chapter 1, GATT contains an existing set of articles that describes under which circumstances trade barriers may be employed. One way to incorporate labour standards in this agreement would be to try to find possibilities of interpreting labour standards in some of the existing articles of GATT. In fact, as we already have noted in the introduction, article XX contains one labour standard – in the list of general exceptions to the free trade principle is mentioned 'products of prison labour'. Another point in the list of general exceptions gives an importing economy the right to adopt 'measures necessary to protect human, animal or plant life or health'. Consequently, this article gives an economy the right to take trade restrictive actions in order to protect human health and life. Obviously, this article is concerned with the situation in the importing rather than the exporting economy. However, it is not impossible to interpret the article, as it stands, as giving a potential protection to all human beings, including those living and working in foreign countries. Direct practical application of such a wide interpretation would certainly meet strong opposition. Leaving practical difficulties aside, we should note that in the recent as well as the much older debate on labour standards and international trade, there have been arguments closely related to the content of a widely interpreted article XX. The fear of foreign competition has been seen as a potential hindrance for making improvements in working conditions in individual economies.

Article XVI of GATT dealing with subsidies can also be interpreted in terms of labour standards. In its first section this article reads: 'If any contracting party grants or maintains any subsidy, including any form of income or price support, which operates directly or indirectly to increase exports of any product from, or to reduce imports of any product into, its territory,' so that 'serious prejudice to the interests of any other contracting party is caused or threatened by any such subsidization, the contracting party granting the subsidy shall, upon request, discuss with the other contracting party or parties concerned, . . . the possibility of limiting the subsidization.' As this article clearly includes all types of export promoting subsidies, it seems consistent also to include special treatments with respect to working condition requirements in the export industry of a country. From a producer's point of view, the ability to keep working conditions at a low level may be equivalent to receiving a direct subsidy when the requirements on working conditions are higher.

The attempt to incorporate labour standards in GATT by employing a wider interpretation of existing GATT articles may be seen as a means of disguising the incorporation *per se*. It may be more straightfoward to work for an explicit incorporation. This can be done either by extending some of the existing GATT articles or by adding a completely new labour standard article, or a social clause, to GATT.

By the safeguard clause, GATT article XIX, a country has the right to restrict its imports of a product if the product 'is being imported into the territory [of the country] in such increased quantities and under such conditions as to cause or threaten serious injury to domestic producers in that territory of like or directly competitive products'. It is further stated that the trade restriction shall be in operation only 'to the extent and for such time as may be necessary to prevent or remedy such injury'. This article indirectly includes the claim that adjustments should take place in the importing country in order that the trade restrictions applied could be withdrawn. It should be noted that the safeguard clause is unconditional with respect to the reasons underlying the increased import competition. In the debate on social clauses there have been proposals for making this article selective with respect to the working conditions in foreign production units. Furthermore, there have been demands implying that if these working conditions are substandard there should be no obligation for adjustments to take place.

An incorporation of labour standards in a revised article XIX will have a clear protectionistic bias since import restrictions may only be applied if domestic producers in the importing country are seriously injured or threatened to be so. The introduction of labour standards in GATT by an extension of the interpretation of article XX, or an extension of the list of general exceptions given in article XX, will contain no such bias. The mere fact that working conditions abroad are below the explicitly stated minimum standards is enough to allow import restrictions to be used. If a completely new labour standard article, or social clause, is added to GATT, nothing can be said in advance about the protectionistic bias without knowing the details of this new article.

Which Labour Standards Should be Included?

Assuming that it is decided that labour standards should be incorporated in GATT, there are some important questions left to be analysed. Which labour standards should be incorporated? Which methods should be adopted?

Let us begin by recalling that the aim of GATT's work is to reduce barriers of trade and pave the way for free trade in order to improve standards of living in the trading economies. The theoretical basis of the struggle for trade liberalisation was developed by Adam Smith, who as early as the eighteenth century presented the theory of absolute advantages.[3] The argument was further developed and strengthened by Robert Torrens and David Ricardo, who formulated the theory of comparative advantages, a theory that still is at the very centre of trade theory.[4]

Smith, Torrens and Ricardo were all representatives of English classical economics that was based heavily on a philosophy of liberalism. Consequently, the argument of free trade can be seen as an offspring of liberalism, in which the freedom of individual economic agents, producers as well as consumers, was the fundamental principle. So, even if GATT does not include any explicit requirements on the freedom of economic agents in the member countries, besides the article on prison labour, it seems reasonable that members of GATT, as well as other countries that advocate and wish to take part in international commercial relations based on the principle of free trade, should also guarantee freedom of their economic agents, including the freedom of assembly. Consequently, from this point of view, the clause on basic trade union rights can be claimed to have an outstanding position among the various social clauses for an incorporation in GATT.

Furthermore, if the aim of social clauses is solidarity with foreign workers, we have found that the clause on basic trade union rights is also of the greatest importance. Due to the solidarity aspect and the close ideological link between basic trade union rights and the free trade principle, an incorporation of a social clause on such rights through a revised article XIX would seem inappropriate. The reason is that this article has a pure protectionistic aim; it can be applied only when the importing country is seriously injured or threatened to be so. The solidarity aspect of the clause is taken better care of by extending article XX or by introducing a completely new article on basic trade union rights into GATT.

The social clauses on various specific working conditions have been found to be doubtful from a solidarity point of view. This is especially the case when the foreign workers concerned have the rights to freely form and act through trade unions. In such cases, clauses on specific working conditions really become of dubious value as a means of solidarity, since they will imply an interference with the opportunities that foreign trade unions have of making collective agreements on behalf of their own preferences, in relation to various specific working conditions. However, as a protectionistic measure and as a means of protecting international trade relations from the increased use of traditional trade barriers, the clauses on specific working conditions can become important. For both these purposes, an extension of article XIX can be chosen for incorporation.

If well defined labour standards on specific working conditions were incorporated in the safeguard clause, GATT article XIX, thereby reducing the frequent use of VERs, we have already mentioned some beneficial consequences that would emerge for the international resource allocation. In particular there will be a reduction in the uncertainty in the world economy. The risks for investors and producers will be reduced compared to the case when discriminatory quotas, such as VERs, are used. Finally, instead of discriminating against the most competitive producer just because they are most competitive, which is often the case when VERs are used, a safeguard clause including labour standards will be non-discriminatory given the incorporated minimum requirements on working conditions. Therefore, given the incorporated labour standards, the most efficient producers will be hit least of all.

Social Clauses and the Development Articles of GATT

One important argument against an incorporation of labour standards in GATT is that they would be an obstacle to economic development in less developed countries. Part IV of GATT deals with trade relations between developed and less developed contracting parties. In article XXXVI we can read that in accordance with the basic objectives of GATT, which aim to raise the standards of living and pave the way for a progressive development of the contracting parties, it is agreed that there is 'need for increased access in the largest possible measure to markets under favourable conditions for processed and manufactured products currently or potentially of particular export interest to less developed contracting parties'.

If there can be assumed to be a positive relationship between an incorporation of labour standards in GATT and the standards of living in developing countries with poor working conditions, there will be no conflict between such an incorporation and the content of Part IV of GATT. The question to be answered is whether there is such a positive relationship. The results of our analysis of a social clause on basic trade union rights tend to support the argument that a positive relationship exists between such basic rights and the standard of living or welfare.

Turning to social clauses on specific working conditions our results would appear to be less positive. In fact, from the point of view of solidarity or standard of living, these clauses were found to be very doubtful. However, it is important to remember that these results were derived under the assumption that the individual export economies satisfied the small country assumption. In Chapter 4, we have found that the negative effects of social clauses are reduced if we abandon this assumption. In fact we noted that there is a possibility that an efficient incorporation of such clauses can give the group of export economies covered by social clauses a sort of 'monopoly power' in trade. Hence, it is also possible that the effects on the national income and the standards of living in these economies will be positive, especially if the current trade barriers against exports from less developed countries are taken into consideration.

Practical Problems Concerning the Incorporation of Labour Standards in GATT – Some Remarks

If agreement could also be obtained on the incorporation of certain labour standards in GATT, several practical problems remain to be solved before the standards can be put into operation. Two important sets of questions are: first, how to make the incorporated standards or clauses operative; and secondly, how to arrange the supervision of the standards and their use in international commercial relations.[5]

To make the incorporated social clauses work efficiently, a precise and operative content must be given to each of them. The relevant conventions and recommendations of the ILO can be used as points of departure for the clauses on hours of work, child labour and occupational health and safety. With regard to the clauses on wages and basic trade union rights, the prospects are less promising.

To determine a reference point for a clause on wages is not a simple matter. Should the clause concentrate on wages or should a broader measure of compensation be the basis of the clause? Should the reference point be national from the point of view of each individual economy or should it be of international character? It is outside the scope of the present study to go into details on these matters. It seems clear from an article on fair labour standards and trade from the late 1960s, where no less than twelve different concepts of fair wages or compensations were reviewed, that it is much more difficult to give a social clause on wages a precise and operative content than is the case with the other clauses on specific working conditions.[6]

Furthermore, the problems of making a social clause on basic trade union rights operative would seem to be considerable. Here the ILO conventions nos. 87 and 98 would seem to be natural reference points. Although the overall content of these conventions is clear, problems obviously exist in making them operative in international commercial relations. In order to reduce or overcome these problems, the ILO and its special freedom of association machinery could be utilised.

Assuming that a solution can be found for the problems involved in making the different social clauses operational, procedures for supervision of the incorporated standards must also be established. To judge from the recent documents on the question of labour standards in trade policy, there would seem to be a central place for close co-operation between GATT and the ILO in this respect. One important characteristic of the different ILO supervision procedures that should be kept in mind when supervising labour standards in GATT is the dominance of flexibility over rigidity. Local conditions and the possibility of making improvements in working conditions should be taken into consideration when determining the precise requirements of individual economies.

Finally, to avoid discretion in the use of the social clauses, procedures similar to those contained in the ILO supervision system should be used to determine which countries and industries are to be covered by the clauses. The 'special list' approach now used by the Committee of Experts to comment on reports and the implementation of ratified conventions could be a useful point of departure.[7]

Summary

If a decision is made to incorporate labour standards in GATT:

(i) GATT article XVI on subsidies could be given a literal interpretation which allows for the inclusion of indirect subsidisation through preferential labour laws for export industries. This article could then be advanced as an acceptable basis for applying trade restrictions against imports produced in production units favoured by this sort of subsidisation.

(ii) A *fair labour standard clause* or a *social clause* consisting of the basic trade union rights could be incorporated by extending GATT article XX on general exceptions or by adding a new clause to GATT.

(iii) An extended safeguard clause on emergency actions, article XIX, could include labour standards on specific working conditions. In the event of market disruption, imports from foreign production units with working conditions below the specified minimum levels would then be restricted first.

Finally, if labour standards are incorporated in GATT an organisation must be set up to supervise complaints concerning these standards. As mentioned earlier, there would seem to be a natural place for close co-operation between GATT and the ILO, both in relation to the need to give the incorporated labour standards a precise and operative content, and to supervise the incorporated standards. There would also seem to be a need for accompanying the incorporation of labour standards in GATT with the incorporation of a clause on labour inspectorate in order that complaints on labour standards could be checked by GATT or the ILO.

5.4 Conclusions

The subject of the present study, labour standards in trade policy, has been under debate since the beginning of the nineteenth century. As outlined earlier, after about a hundred years of proposals and conferences, the International Labour Organisation (ILO), was formed in 1919. However, all countries are not members of this organisation. Furthermore, the constitution of the ILO does not contain any explicit links between working conditions and trade policy. Consequently, the demands for an incorporation of labour standards, or social clauses, in the rules that govern international trade have continued, and during the last decade have indeed become quite frequent.

Three groups of motives or aims regarding the incorporation of social clauses in trade policy have been advanced. To recapitulate, these aims are:

(1) To provide protection to domestic industries and workers in the 'old' industrial countries.
(2) To represent an action of solidarity with workers who are at present working under 'unacceptably low' working conditions.
(3) To protect the international 'free trade system' from increased protectionism based on traditional trade barriers.

In the present study, we have concentrated on the economic effects that could be expected to arise if labour standards or social clauses were incorporated in the rules that govern international trade. In addition to an analysis of the incorporation of labour standards carried out in isolation from other trade policy measures, this study also contains a comparative analysis of social clauses on the one hand and tariffs, import quotas and so called 'voluntary export restraints', VERs, on the other.

From these analyses it has been possible to arrive at the following conclusions:

> An incorporation of a social clause on basic trade union rights may be characterised as an action of solidarity with foreign workers that do not have such rights. However, as a protective measure, the value of this type of social clause is doubtful. Nevertheless, the introduction of such a clause can be expected to reduce the demand for traditional protectionist measures.

The following conclusions have been derived with regard to social clauses on specific working conditions:

> They are of dubious value as a means of solidarity with foreign workers. Although some workers may become better off, these gains must be weighed against the losses of other workers in the form of lower wages or unemployment. However, if social clauses affect the price of the commodity in question or reduce the use of other trade policy measures these negative effects will be curtailed. In fact, if it can be assumed that the incorporation of social clauses on specific working conditions provides the export economies concerned with a sort of 'monopoly power' in trade, it is possible that the effects may become positive.
>
> Social clauses on hours of work and child labour are of doubtful value as a protective measure, especially when they are directed against economies that can be characterised as labour surplus economies. Clauses on wages and occupational health and safety are much better suited for this purpose.

By comparing the protective social clauses with traditional trade barriers that are designed in a discriminatory manner in order to yield the same quantity of imports from a specific foreign source, it has been concluded that:

> An importing economy prefers tariffs to social clauses, as well as to the other measures considered, whereas social clauses will never be inferior to VERs from the static point of view of

economic welfare.

A non-discriminated export economy, which yields a surplus from exports of 'clause-covered' commodities, would tend to prefer VERs and import quotas to social clauses and tariffs, unless there is an import monopoly in the importing economy.

A discriminated economy, i.e. an economy that must change the working conditions in the production of commodities covered by the clause in order to comply with the incorporated standards, would tend to prefer VERs to social clauses as well as to tariffs and import quotas. However, workers in the 'clause-covered' industry would tend to prefer social clauses to other trade policy measures. This is especially the case in labour surplus economies and when short run effects are given high priority.

From an international resource allocation point of view, an incorporation of social clauses in GATT can be expected to have important positive effects, provided that the incorporation becomes efficient. The frequent use of VERs can be expected to become less prevalent when social clauses are introduced. Furthermore, the functioning of social clauses has great similarities with that of tariffs.

Hence, it can be concluded that the likelihood of making a social clause on specific working conditions efficient, in the sense that working conditions will come to comply with the stated requirements, increases if the alternative to changes in working conditions is a tariff in the international market.

Finally, it has been noted that if it is decided to introduce social clauses in GATT, close co-operation between this organisation and the ILO would seem to be called for, in order to reduce the practical problems of making the clauses operative and efficient.

Notes

1. ILO (1980), p. 5. See also Chapter 1 of the present study.
2. For instance, see Bergsten (1975), p. 239.
3. Smith (1776).
4. Torrens (1815) and Ricardo (1817).
5. See also Edgren (1979), pp. 526f.
6. Schwenger (1967).
7. See ILO (1978), Ch. 6.

REFERENCES

Alston, P. (1981) 'Commodity Agreement – As Though People Don't Matter', *Journal of World Trade Law*, vol. 15

Arrow, K.J. (1975) 'Gifts and Exchange' in E.S. Phelps (ed.), *Altruism, Morality and Economic Theory*, Russell Sage Foundation, New York

Axelsson, M. and B. Perjus (1978) *Asien* in *Facklig Horisont* (Series), Prisma, Lund

Balassa, B. (1978) 'The "New Protectionism" and the International Economy', *Journal of World Trade Law*, vol. 12

Baldwin, R.E. (1980) *The Political Economy of Protectionism*, National Bureau Conference on Import Competition and Adjustment: Theory and Policy, 8–11 May 1980, Cambridge, Mass. (Xeroxed)

Batra, R.N. and A.C. Seth (1977) 'Unemployment, Tariffs and the Theory of International Trade', *Journal of International Economics*, vol. 7

Baumol, W.J. (1971) *Environmental Protection, International Spillovers and Trade*, Wicksell Lectures 1971, Almqvist & Wiksell, Stockholm

Bentzel, R. and Ö. Johansson (1959) 'Om homogenitet i produktionsfunktioner', *Ekonomisk Tidskrift*

Bergsten, C.F. (1975) 'On the Non-equivalence of Import Quotas, and "Voluntary" Export Restraints' in C.F. Bergsten (ed.), *Toward a New World Trade Policy: The Maidenhead Papers*, Lexington Books, Lexington, Mass.

Bhagwati, J. (1965) 'On the Equivalence of Tariffs and Quotas' in R.E. Baldwin *et al.* (eds.), *Trade, Growth and the Balance of Payments*, Rand McNally, Chicago

——— (1968) 'More on the Equivalence of Tariffs and Quotas', *American Economic Review*, vol. 58

——— (1971) 'The Generalized Theory of Distortions and Welfare' in J. Bhagwati *et al.* (eds.), *Trade, Balance of Payments and Growth*, North Holland, Amsterdam

Bhagwati, J., V.K. Ramaswami and T.N. Srinivasan (1969) 'Domestic Distortions, Tariffs and the Theory of Optimum Subsidy: Some Further Results', *Journal of Political Economy*, vol. 77

Blanpain, R. (ed.) (1979) *International Encyclopaedia for Labour Law and Industrial Relations*, Kluwer, The Netherlands

Blaug, M. (1963) 'A Survey of the Theory of Process-Innovations', *Economica*, vol. 30

Blum S. (1925) *Labor Economics*, Henry Holt and Company, New York

Braun, K. (1950) *The Right to Organize and Its Limits*, The Brookings Institution, Washington, DC

Brecher, R.A. (1974) 'Minimum Wage Rates and the Pure Theory of International Trade', *Quarterly Journal of Economics*, vol. 88

Brock, W.A. and S.P. Magee (1978) 'The Economics of Special Interest Politics: The Case of Tariffs', *American Economic Review*, vol. 68

Brown, C. and J. Medoff (1978) 'Trade Unions in the Production Process', *Journal of Political Economy*, vol. 86

Burenstam-Linder, S. (1980) 'How to Avoid a New International Economic Disorder', *World Economy*, vol. 3

Burton, J. (1978) 'Are Trade Unions a Public Good/Bad? The Economics of the Closed Shop' in *Trade Unions – Public Goods or Public Bads?*, The Institute of Economic Affairs, London

Caire, G. (1977) *Freedom of Association and Economic Development*, ILO, Geneva

del Castillo, E.A. (1979) 'Mexico' in R. Blanpain (ed.), *International Encyclopaedia for Labour Law and Industrial Relations*, Kluwer, The Netherlands

Cesarino, Jr, A.F. and M.A. Cardone (1979) 'Brazil' in R. Blanpain (ed.), *International Encyclopaedia for Labour Law and Industrial Relations*, Kluwer, The Netherlands

China, Republic of (1979) *Statistical Yearbook of the Republic of China*

Clark, K.B. (1980) 'Unionization and Productivity: Micro-Econometric Evidence', *Quarterly Journal of Economics*, vol. 95

Department of Labour, Canada (1979) *International Fair Labour Standards: Some Issues*, mimeo, April 1979

Drèze, J.H. (1976) 'Some Theory of Labor Management and Participation', *Econometrica*, vol. 44

Dunlop, J. (1958) *Industrial Relations Systems*, Southern Illinois University Press, Carbondale

Edgren, G. (1979) 'Fair Labour Standards and Trade Liberalisation', *International Labour Review*, vol. 118

EEC Economic and Social Committee (1980) *Report of the Section for External Relations on Development Cooperation and the Economic and Social Consequences of Applying Certain International Standards Governing Working Conditions*, Brussels

Erstling, J.A. (1977) *The Right to Organize*, ILO, Geneva

European Parliament (1977) *Bulletin 78/2*, Dec. 1977

The European Social Charter and International Labour Standards I and II (1961) *International Labour Review*, vol. 84

Feis, H. (1927) 'International Labour Legislation in the Light of Economic Theory', *International Labour Review*, vol. 15

Fishelson, G and F. Flatters (1975) 'The (Non)Equivalence of Optimal Tariffs and Quotas under Uncertainty', *Journal of International Economics*, vol. 5

Follows, J.W. (1951) *Antecedents of the International Labour Organization*, Clarendon Press, Oxford

Franklin, N.N. (1969) 'Minimum-Wage Fixing and Economic Development' in A.D. Smith (ed.), *Wage Policy Issues in Economic Development*, Macmillan, London

Freeman, R.B. (1976) 'Individual Mobility and Union Voice in the Labor Market', *American Economic Review*, vol. 66

Fröbel, F. *et al.* (1977) *Die neue internationale Arbeitsteilung*, Rowohlt Taschenbuch Verlag GmbH, Hamburg

Galenson, W. (1959) *Labour and Economic Development*, John Wiley & Sons, New York

Gard, L.M. and J. Riedel (1980) 'Safeguard Protection of Industry in Developed Countries: Assessment of the Implications for Developing Countries', *Weltwirtschaftliches Archiv*, Band 116

GATT (1971) *Industrial Pollution Control and International Trade*, GATT Studies in International Trade No. 1, Geneva

——— (1973) *Handelsdepartementet*, Allmänna Förlaget, Stockholm

Graham, F. (1948) *The Theory of International Values*, Princeton University Press, Princeton, NJ

Gruen, F.H. and W.M. Corden (1970) 'A Tariff that Worsens the Terms of Trade' in I.A. McDougall and R.H. Snape (eds.), *Studies in International Economics*, North Holland, Amsterdam

Haas, E.B. (1970) *Human Rights and International Action*, Stanford University Press, Stanford, California

Hamilton, C. (1975) 'Increased Child Labour – An External Diseconomy of Rural Employment Creation for Adults', *Asian*

Economies
Hamilton, C. (1978a) 'Ska Sverige exportera sin arbetslöshet till u-länderna? *Tiden*, no. 3/4
——— (1978b) 'Argumenten för frihandeln kvarstår', *Tiden*, no. 6
Hansson, G. (1982) 'Do Trade Unions Really Give Rise to Social Losses?', *Statsvetenskaplig Tidskrift*, no. 1
Hansson, G. and M. Lundahl (1981a) *A Social Clause against Discrimination in the Labor Market*, mimeo, Lund
——— (1981b) *The Rybczynski Theorem under Decreasing Returns to Scale*, mimeo, Lund
Hicks, J.R. (1932) *The Theory of Wages*, Macmillan, London
ICFTU (1979) *1980 Review of the World Economic Situation*, Brussels
ILO, (1956) *Social Aspects of European Economic Co-operation*, ILO, Geneva
——— (1968) *Minimum Wage Fixing and Economic Development*, ILO, Geneva
——— (1971) *Freedom of Association for Workers' and Employers' Organisations and Their Role in Social and Economic Development*, Report III, Seventh Asian Regional Conference, Teheran
——— (1975) *Freedom of Association, an International Survey*, ILO, Geneva
——— (1978) *International Labour Standards*, ILO, Geneva
——— (1980) *Constitution of the International Labour Organisation and Standing Orders of the International Labour Conference*, Geneva
IMF (1978) *The Rise in Protectionism*, IMF Pamphlet Series no. 24, Washington, DC
The Independent Commission on International Development Issues (1980) *North-South: A Programme for Survival* (the Brandt Report), Pan Books, London
Jenks, C.W. (1960) *Human Rights and International Labour Standards*, London Institute of World Affairs, Stevens & Sons Limited, London
Johnson, H.G. (1969) 'Minimum Wage Laws: A General Equilibrium Analysis', *Canadian Journal of Economics*, vol. 2
Johnson, H.G., P. Wonnacott, and H. Shibata (1968) *Harmonization of National Economic Policies under Free Trade*, University of Toronto Press, Toronto

Jones, R.W. (1971) 'Distortions in Factor Markets and the General Equilibrium Model of Production', *Journal of Political Economy*, vol. 79

——— (1977) *'Two-Ness' in Trade Theory: Costs and Benefits*, Special Papers in International Economics, no. 12, Princeton University, Princeton, NJ

Kassalow, E.M. (1969) *Trade Unions and Industrial Relations: An International Comparison*, New York

Kochin, L.A. (1980) 'The Social Cost of Union Monopoly', *Statsvetenskaplig Tidskrift*, no. 5

Korea, Republic of (1980) *Korea Statistical Yearbook*

Krawtschenko, N. (1910) 'J.A. Blanqui – der erste Verkünder der Idee des internationalen Arbeiterschutzes', *Jahrbücher für Nationalekonomie und Statistik*, vol. 40

Kreinin, M.E. (1970) 'More on the Equivalence of Tariffs and Quotas', *Kyklos*, vol. 23

Kullmann, U. (1980) '"Fair Labour Standards" in International Commodity Agreements', *Journal of World Trade Law*, vol. 14

Landsorganisationen i Sverige (1980) *Facket och de nya industriländerna: En rapport från LOs Ostasiendelegation* in *Facklig Horisont* (Series), Prisma, Stockholm

Lester, R.A. (1969) *Economics of Labor*, 2nd ed, The Macmillan Company, New York

Lethbridge, D.C. and N.S. Hong (1979) 'Hong Kong' in R. Blanpain (ed.), *International Encyclopaedia for Labour Law and Industrial Relations*, Kluwer, The Netherlands

Lewis, W.A. (1954) 'Economic Development with Unlimited Supplies of Labour', *The Manchester School*, vol. 22

Lindsay, S.M. (1934) 'The Problem of American Cooperation' in J.T. Shotwell (ed.), *The Origins of the International Labor Organization*, vol. I, Columbia University Press, New York

LO and TCO (1978) *Skyddsklausulfrågor i de multilaterala handelsförhandlingarna i GATT*, Skrivelse till Statsrådet och Chefen för Handelsdepartementet

Long, O. (1977) 'The Protectionist Threat to World Trade Relations', *Intereconomics*, no. 11/12

——— (1978) 'International Trade under Threat, a Constructive Response', *World Economy*, vol. 1

Luard, E. (ed.) (1967) *The International Protection of Human Rights*, Thames and Hudson, London

Lundahl, M. (1979) 'Tillväxt och kapitalbildning i femtiotalets

utvecklingsekonomi: Några viktiga teorier' in M. Lundahl and B. Södersten (eds.), *Utvecklingsekonomi*, Bonniers, Stockholm
McCulloch, R. (1973) 'When are a Tariff and a Quota Equivalent?', *Canadian Journal of Economics*, vol. 6
Magee, S.P. (1973) 'Factor Market Distortions, Production, and Trade: A Survey', *Oxford Economic Papers*, vol. 25
Mahaim, E. (1934) 'The Historical and Social Importance of International Labor Legislation' in J.T. Shotwell (ed.), *The Origins of the International Labor Organization*, vol. I, Columbia University Press, New York
Mayer, W. (1974) 'Short-Run and Long-Run Equilibrium for a Small Open Economy', *Journal of Political Economy*, vol. 82
Mehta, A. (1957) 'The Mediating Role of the Trade Union in Underdeveloped Countries', *Economic Development and Cultural Change*, vol. 6
Meier, G.M. (1976) *Leading Issues in Economic Development*, 3rd edn, Oxford University Press, New York
Mendelievich, E. (ed.) (1979) *Children at Work*, ILO, Geneva
Mintzes, J. (1960) 'Union Views on Fair Labor Standards in Foreign Trade', *Monthly Labor Review*, vol. 83
Mortensen, D. (1970) 'A Theory of Wage and Employment Dynamics' in E. Phelps (ed.), *Microeconomic Foundations of Employment and Inflation Theory*, W.W. Norton and Co., New York
Nath, S. (1969) *A Reappraisal of Welfare Economics*, Routledge & Kegan Paul, London
Negishi, T. (1972) *General Equilibrium Theory and International Trade*, North Holland, Amsterdam
Olson, M. (1965) *The Logic of Collective Action: Public Goods and the Theory of Groups*, Harvard University Press, Cambridge, Mass.
Owen, R. (1857/8) *The Life of Robert Owen*, vol. I, IA, Effingham Wilson, London
Parker, C.H. (1920) *The Casual Laborer and Other Essays*, Harcourt, Brace and Howe, New York
Pelcovits, M.D. (1976) 'Quotas versus Tariffs', *Journal of International Economics*, vol. 6
Phelan, E.J. (1934) 'British Preparations' in J.T. Shotwell (ed.), *The Origins of the International Labor Organization*, vol. I, Columbia University Press, New York
Phelps, E.S. (ed.) (1975) Introduction to *Altruism, Morality and*

Economic Theory, Russell Sage Foundation, New York

Picquenard, C. (1934) 'French Preparations' in J.T. Shotwell (ed.), *The Origins of the International Labor Organization*, vol. I, Columbia University Press, New York

Pincus, J.J. (1975) 'Pressure Groups and the Pattern of Tariffs', *Journal of Political Economy*, vol. 83

Porter, R. (1975) 'Child Labour in Hong Kong and Related Problems: A Brief Review', *International Labour Review*, vol. 111

Posner, R.A. (1975) 'The Social Cost of Monopoly and Regulation', *Journal of Political Economy*, vol. 83

Proposal Concerning a Social Clause to be Inserted in the G.A.T.T. Treaty (1976) International Metalworkers' Federation, February 1976

Proposal on Minimum International Labour Standards (1979) US submission to the GATT, October 1979

Rawls, J. (1973) *A Theory of Justice*, Oxford University Press, London

Rees, A. (1962) *The Economics of Trade Unions*, University of Chicago Press, Chicago

Reynolds, M.O. (1981) 'Whatever Happened to the Monopoly Theory of Labor Unions?', *Journal of Labor Research*, vol. 2

Ricardo, D. (1817) *Principles of Political Economy and Taxation*, printed for John Murray, London

Robbins, L. (1978) 'Economics and Trade Unions, 1776–1977' in *Trade Unions – Public Goods or Public Bads?*, The Institute of Economic Affairs, London

Robson P. (1980) *The Economics of International Integration*, George Allen & Unwin, London

Rodriguez, C.A. (1974) 'The Non-equivalence of Tariffs and Quotas under Retaliation', *Journal of International Economics*, vol. 4

Rybczynski, T.M. (1955) 'Factor Endowments and Relative Commodity Prices', *Economica*, vol. 22

Sampson, G.P. (1980) 'Contemporary Protectionism and Exports of Developing Countries', *World Development*, vol. 8

Samuelson, P.A. (1954) 'The Pure Theory of Public Expenditures', *Review of Economics and Statistics*, vol. 36

Sanger, S. (1920) 'Practical Problems of International Labour Legislation', Ch. VI in E.J. Solano (ed.), *Labour as an International Problem*, Macmillan & Co., London

Säve-Söderbergh, B. (1978a) 'U-länderna, frihandeln och jobben', *Tiden*, no. 2

——— (1978b) 'Replik till Hamilton', *Tiden*, no. 5

deSchweinitz Jr, K. (1959) 'Industrialization, Labor Controls and Democracy', *Economic Development and Cultural Change*, vol. 8

Schwenger, R.B. (1967) 'Fair Labor Standards for World Trade', *Monthly Labor Review*, vol. 90

Shibata, H. (1968) 'A Note on the Equivalence of Tariffs and Quotas', *American Economic Review*, vol. 58

Shotwell, J.T. (ed.) (1934) *The Origins of the International Labor Organization*, vol. I, Columbia University Press, New York

Slichter, S., J. Healy and E.R. Livernash (1960) *The Impact of Collective Bargaining on Management*, Brookings Institution, Washington, DC

Smith, A. (1776) *The Wealth of Nations* (Pelican Classics, Penguin, Harmondsworth 1973)

Smith, A.D. (1967) 'Minimum Wages and the Distribution of Income with Special Reference to Developing Countries', *International Labour Review*, vol. 96

Södersten, B. (1964) *A Study of Economic Growth and International Trade*, Almqvist & Wiksell, Stockholm

——— (1980) *International Economics*, 2nd edn, Macmillan Press, London

Solano, E.J. (1920) *Labour as an International Problem*, Macmillan & Co, London

Starr, G. (1981) 'Minimum Wage Fixing: International Experience with Alternative Roles', *International Labour Review*, vol. 120

Stolper, W. and P.A. Samuelson (1941) 'Protection and Real Wages', *Review of Economic Studies*, vol. 9

Sturmthal, A. (1960) 'Unions and Economic Development', *Economic Development and Cultural Change*, vol. 9

Takacs, W.E. (1978) 'The Non-equivalence of Tariffs, Import Quotas, and Voluntary Export Restraints', *Journal of International Economics*, vol. 8

Torrens, R. (1815) *Essay on the External Corn Trade*, printed for J. Hatchard, London

Tower, E. (1975) 'The Optimum Quota and Retaliation', *Review of Economic Studies*, vol. 42

Tullock, G. (1967) 'The Welfare Costs of Tariffs, Monopolies, and Theft', *Western Economic Journal*, vol. 4

Udviklingssamarbejde og Overholdelse af visse Internationale Normer for Arbejdsvilkår, (1978) KOM (78) 492, Brussels

UN (1948) *United Nations Conference on Trade and Employment*, Havana, UN Doc. E/Conf. 2/78 (1948), Article 7(1)

UNCTAD (1978) *Growing Protectionism and the Standstill on Trade Barriers against Imports from Developing Countries* (TD/B/C.2/194), UNCTAD, Geneva

US Department of Labor, Bureau of International Labor Affairs (1978) *Labor Standards and Trade Distortions*, mimeo, Washington, DC, September 1978

US Department of Labor, Bureau of Labor Statistics (1920) *Historical Survey on International Action Affecting Labor*, Government Printing Office, Washington, DC

——— (1981) *Estimated Hourly Compensation of Production Workers in 34 Manufacturing Industries, 31 Countries, 1979*, unpublished

US Tariff Act of 1930 (1930) Washington, DC

Utrikesutskottets betänkande (1978/9) *Riktlinjer för Internationellt Utvecklingssamarbete m.m.*, 1978/79:1

Valticos, N. (1979) 'International Labour Law' in R. Blanpain (ed.), *International Encyclopaedia for Labour Law and Industrial Relations*, Kluwer, The Netherlands

Vastrup, C. (1979) 'The Choice between a Tariff and a Quota under Uncertainty', *Welwirtschaftliches Archiv*, vol. 115

Viscusi, W.K. (1979) 'Job Hazards and Worker Quit Rates: An Analysis of Adaptive Work Behavior', *International Economic Review*, vol. 20

——— (1980) 'Union, Labor Market Structure, and the Welfare Implications of the Quality of Work', *Journal of Labor Research*, vol. 1

Walter, I. (1971) 'On the Equivalence of Tariffs and Quotas: a Comment', *Kyklos*, vol. 24

Watanabe, S. (1976) 'Minimum Wages in Developing Countries: Myth and Reality', *International Labour Review*, vol. 113

Webb, S. and B. (1902) *Industrial Democracy*, Longmans, London

Yadav, G.J. (1968) 'A Note on the Equivalence of Tariffs and Quotas', *Canadian Journal of Economics*, vol. 1

Yearbook of Labour Statistics (various issues) ILO, Geneva

Yearbook of Labour Statistics (various issues) Republic of China

INDEX

Made in the USA
Las Vegas, NV
04 May 2026

dac25042-943b-4070-9f5e-023395540a30R02